CHOOSING EACH OTHER EVERY DAY

Heartfelt and Humorous Conversations on the Art of Marriage

Choosing Each Other Every Day

Heartfelt and Humorous Conversations on the Art of Marriage

Jodie and Reggie Howard

©2025 All Rights Reserved. No portion of this book may be reproduced, stored in a retrieval system, or transmitted in any form or by any means—electronic, mechanical, photocopy, recording, scanning, or other—except for brief quotations in critical reviews or articles without the prior permission of the author.

Published by Game Changer Publishing

Paperback ISBN: 978-1-966659-47-1

Hardcover ISBN: 978-1-966659-73-0

Digital ISBN: 978-1-966659-48-8

www.GameChangerPublishing.com

DEDICATION

To our younger selves for trusting that their love could carry them through whatever came their way and for always choosing each other.

READ THIS FIRST

Just to say thanks for buying and reading our book, we would like to give you an exclusive personal welcome as you begin this journey with us!

Scan the QR Code:

CHOOSING EACH OTHER EVERY DAY

Heartfelt and Humorous Conversations on the Art of Marriage

FOREWORD

I was a big fan of fairy tales growing up. We're a big Disney family, and I spent so much of my childhood mesmerized by these stories. From Cinderella's glass slipper to the Beast gifting Belle a magical library to Buttercup being rescued by Wesley, these love stories followed me. For a long time, I thought they were what shaped my understanding of love and relationships.

But as I got older and stepped out into the world, I realized that the real-life love story that I had grown up witnessing was far more powerful than any fairytale. My parents, Jodie and Reggie, have spent my entire lifetime choosing each other. As you read the pages of this book, you'll hear their story. You'll learn how they navigated an unexpected pregnancy (aka, me). They'll share how they navigated falling in love young and how they moved through life in the military. You'll hear stories about my siblings and the unique gift they've each brought to our family.

You'll get a taste of my parent's dynamic, how they laugh, banter, and call each other out. And while I'm really happy for you

FOREWORD

that you'll get to witness this, I would be remiss if I didn't tell you that this book isn't even the half of it.

I'd be remiss if I didn't tell you that I don't know if anything can really capture my parents—their love, devotion, and playfulness. I don't know if there are enough words to describe how watching them has shaped how my siblings and I move through the world. They are a living embodiment of what is possible when it comes to love.

You have your own love story; I don't know what it is. But I hope, and I know my parents hope this as well, that as you read these pages, you are reminded that love is a sacred holy thing—it's also a real devotional choice. And that you are worthy of a love that sees you, and teases you, and excites you, and challenges you.

In reading my parents' story and my family's story, I hope you walk away knowing that your love is enough and that this love is just as available to you as it has been to them and to us.

Happy reading, and with only more love,

– Olivia Howard

CONTENTS

INTRODUCTION	xv
LOVE AT FIRST SIGHT?	1
GUESS WHO'S COMING TO DINNER?	23
OUR ROARING TWENTIES	41
SPECIAL BLESSINGS	59
FORGING A NEW PATH... TOGETHER	75
NO FOX LIKE A MAD FOX	93
LUCY IN THE SKY, LILY IN THE FIELD	107
BAHRAIN AND BEYOND	125
THE AFTERLIFE	143
CONCLUSION: MARRYING WELL	161
REFERENCES	165
NOTES	167
WE HOPE YOU ENJOYED READING OUR BOOK!	169

Reggie: It's the number one rule in life: Marry well or don't marry at all.

Jodie: According to Reggie, that is...

Reggie: According to anyone who's actually happy in life *and* marriage. It's the essence of what we're trying to get across in this book.

Jodie: How many times have you shared that rule of yours?

Reggie: Not enough.

Jodie: But what does it actually mean to *marry well?*

Reggie: It's different for everyone, but there are fundamental truths that apply to all. As we move through this book together, our goal and hope is to reflect upon those fundamentals and the core principles of what it means to *marry well*. The one thing we've both learned in this life is that having a partner you can collaborate with, connect with, and get crazy with is the recipe for something special.

Jodie: I actually agree with you, but I often give you a hard time about this favorite saying of yours because... well, it can feel a little trite.

Reggie: Not trite; it's simple. All the great things in life are simple.

Jodie: *All* great things?

Reggie: Except you, of course. You are anything but simple.

Jodie: Thank you. I do think there's a lot more depth to that saying than I give it credit.

Reggie: It's kinda like me. When people first meet me, they don't realize how much depth is actually there.

Jodie: [laughs] Yes, it is *very* much like you.

Reggie: I'm not just your basic cup of coffee. I'm an espresso with a hint of blackberries, currants, and cinnamon, and it's only when you taste it and savor it that all those depths and flavors start coming through. I'm *that* kind of espresso, the "me" espresso.
Jodie: [chuckles] True. And truly, I do love that kind of espresso...I've been savoring it for more than three decades now!

INTRODUCTION

How did a Southern man from Macon, Georgia, who attended the Naval Academy and started a life in Navy service, meet an intelligent, vibrant, spicy woman from Miami, Florida? How did they build a life and stay together for over thirty years (and counting)? Jodie and Reggie would say that the universe brought them together. Their souls have been on this journey for a long, long time, and this is the iteration of how their relationship is meant to be—right here, right now, in this lifetime. But even if the universe brought them together, they experienced the pleasure and trials of figuring out how to actually *stay* connected and together.

What is the secret to staying together all these years? Jodie and Reggie have remained true to each other, despite all the trials and tribulations life has brought to their doorstep—from being an interracial couple to an unexpected pregnancy, the stress of a military lifestyle, the strain of being in a long-distance relationship, having a child with significant special needs, and facing unexpected loss and grief. They've seen it all, but through it all, they continue to choose each other. Although it's often messy, and they've lost their way from time to time, at the core of their beings, they *choose* each other. Their motto for marrying well: "We choose *us*."

Jodie and Reggie have learned that in order to choose each other and be fully present in a relationship, they must first take the time to learn about themselves. Understanding who they are, why they do the things they do, and how they move through the world as individuals has proven vital in sustaining their deep connection with each other. Becoming aware of limiting beliefs, personality types, and natal tendencies is essential in a healthy and happy lifelong partnership. With this knowledge, they were able to create more space and grace for themselves, and, in turn, they had more space and grace for each other.

In the ongoing process of *choosing us*, Jodie and Reggie also learned to continually *choose themselves*. They needed to understand what made them tick as individuals, which added a depth to their relationship in a way they never expected. It has also deepened their appreciation for each other, allowing their individual strengths and abilities to reach greater heights. They recognize each other's blind spots, so they can readily step in and assist.

———

> **Reggie**: We've been in love and have known each other for thirty-something years now.
> **Jodie:** That's a long time!
> **Reggie**: While it doesn't seem like a long time for me, I know it seems like a lifetime for you.
> **Jodie:** Ha-ha!
> **Reggie**: We've grown and changed, experienced heartache

and joy, learned about ourselves and each other, and we've done it all together.

Jodie: It hasn't always been pretty, but it has always been *us*. It all starts with *us* and ends with *us*. And when we *choose us,* we can get through anything that life throws our way.

Reggie: We're ready to share our story. We've gotten through some really tough challenges and actually came out stronger on the other side.

Jodie: We're writing this book for anyone who's in a relationship, whether you're married, contemplating marriage, or even contemplating a relationship.

Reggie: Actually, I think we wrote this book because you told me we needed to write it.

Jodie: [Ha!] I'm pretty sure you told *me* we needed to do this, and you got the ball rolling.

Reggie: That's because I know our story has something for everyone. It's not just for couples who have been together for a long time; it's also for those new relationships. Plus, there's that feeling of, *If only I'd known so many of these things sooner.* That would've helped *me* so much to process and understand what was going on between *us*.

Jodie: *If only...* I hear you. But I believe the tools come to us when we are ready for them. We have to be open to receiving them before they can make a difference. I believe we learn our lessons exactly when we are meant to.

Reggie: Yes, it's time to share our insights, which may help others with their own realizations.

Jodie: To be clear, this isn't a marriage how-to book.

Reggie: Um, yeah, it is. I'm here to tell our readers how-to and how-*not*-to.

Jodie: I know *you* are. But this book isn't an actual guide to marriage. Rather, it's us telling our story and what we believe is possible in a relationship. We share our ups and downs, how we've made it through, but the takeaway message is that marrying well can be achieved.

Reggie: Absolutely, it can be done.

Jodie: After thirty years of marriage, it's possible to not only love each other but to really *like* each other.

Reggie: That's not what most of the world wanted us to think.

Jodie: I believe that when you continually choose each other and do it in your own way, you can get to the place you want to go—together.

Reggie: And we're gonna share some of those tools—the ones you're always telling me about, like my "Penthouse" Moon sign and your "Mani-Pedi" Energy, and all those books you've made me read, right?

Jodie: [Laughing] Maybe one day you'll get the names right?!—since there is no such thing as a "Penthouse" Moon or "Mani-Pedi" Energy. But, yes, we will discuss our natal Moon signs, along with our varying energy and personality Types, our Love Languages, and how they have each influenced and affected our relationship.

Reggie: Good. I'll see if I can keep the names straight. But either way, there are some great tips in these pages. We've been on an interesting journey so far. I hope everyone will enjoy the ride!

―――――

Jodie and Reggie met during a chance encounter in the summer of 1990, never imagining everything life would throw at them, much less that they'd one day write a book about it. Their intention in writing this book is to share their stories and explore their deep emotional connection. This is your invitation to pull up a chair, settle in, and join Jodie and Reggie on their journey. Read these words with an open mind and heart.

Throughout this book, Jodie and Reggie share many tools that have made all the difference in their lives and their relationship. They hope you will gain valuable insight about how to marry well. Each chapter offers an intimate glimpse into their personal experiences, revealing the heart and soul of their journey: Trust yourself and trust the process. When you truly know yourself, you can embrace all your strengths and weaknesses and learn how to coexist with your partner on a foundation of love. There are so many beautiful possibilities out there waiting for you.

LOVE AT FIRST SIGHT?

Does the highly romanticized story of love at first sight actually exist? Or is it merely a fabrication of fairy tales and Hallmark movies? Many people believe they've experienced love at first sight, only to realize it was actually lust or some variation that ended up falling terribly short of true love.

For Jodie and Reggie, love at first sight does exist, but their vision of love has changed from year to year, month to month, and even minute by minute. The tricky part wasn't discovering love at first sight but *uncovering* how to make that first sight last a lifetime.

Jodie: Do you believe in love at first sight?
Reggie: Yeah, I do.
Jodie: Do you think we experienced love at first sight?
Reggie: I definitely believe we had love at first sight. I still remember the moment when I first saw you. I was

working at O'Charley's when I saw you and thought, *Damn, stop the press! Who is this, and how do I get to know her?*
Jodie: Okay, but was that love or something else?
Reggie: Yes, it was love. And it was something else! It was that thing—that spark—that needs to be present at the beginning of any relationship. There has to be a spark of interest that makes you want to learn more about the person. In my case, I *needed* to know more.

———

When I first met Jodie in 1990, I was a young Ensign in the Navy and had just started my naval career. I was going through flight school and had three months of downtime before my next training. Every morning at 6:00 a.m., I would perform my one daily military obligation: Call the front office desk of the military command and inquire if they needed me that day. Most days, the answer was no, so I would hang up, roll back over in bed, and return to my alcohol-induced coma. I was barhopping every night of the week in Pensacola, Florida, where my command was located. I was twenty-three and had the whole world ahead of me.

Pensacola is where all aspiring naval aviators begin their initial training. It is known for its beautiful beaches and scenic, original-themed bars. Upon my arrival, it became one of my missions to live by the motto, "Work hard, play hard," just like I had seen in Top Gun. *During this hold in my training, I discovered every alcohol- and dance-fused bar and club in town. I knew where to be from Monday to Sunday, and after a while, every bartender and bouncer knew me by name. I was like Norm from* Cheers *in quite a few establishments on the Gold Coast.*

Life was great for a month or so, but eventually, I grew bored. I wanted to do something else to change up my day, so I decided to get another job. Since I didn't have any set responsibilities with my Navy job, I had plenty of time and energy for another gig. My friend, Monya, helped me get hired as a waiter at O'Charley's (think Ruby Tuesday or TGI Friday's). That was still one of the best jobs I ever had because it was a job I didn't need. You can have a lot of fun when you don't care if you get fired. The rules were definitely advisory, and everything was fun and games. I made some serious tip money because I had a deal set up with the hostesses: Any table of more than four women was put in my section. I gave my customers a performance, and I made about $200 in tips every five-hour shift, which was serious cash back then. My Navy salary paid my bills, so most of my tip money was put back into the local P-Cola economy via the bars and clubs that I frequented with my crew, buying everyone rounds and shots on my O'Charley's income. I have fond memories of mind erasers and Depeche Mode, but I digress.

Everything changed on the day Jodie walked into O'Charley's. I was walking out of the kitchen, carrying a tray with main course meals for eight customers. I literally froze in my tracks. While holding the platter—plates of food sizzling in my ear—I had a five-minute conversation with this beautiful woman. She told me she was in town for the weekend, visiting Monya. Afterward, I rushed to a payphone and called my roommate, Steve, to tell him that I thought I had just met the One! I didn't know at the time where this vision had come from. All I knew was that I wanted—no, needed—to know more about her.

Later that night, as the staff was rolling silverware, Jodie and Monya returned. Jodie sat next to me in a group of six people. We were talking and laughing until this highly inebriated young man came over to the table holding a yard glass filled with beer. He gazed at Jodie and made some not-so-subtle suggestions about the "magic" the two of them could make together.

I slid close to Jodie and put my arm around her shoulder. I looked the dude up and down and said, "Your best chance for magic tonight is *with that glass in your hand because this beautiful girl is with me tonight and every night. Now I don't want to whup your ass, but I will if you say one more word to her. Have a good night."*

As he walked away, I pulled my arm away, but Jodie stopped me and gave me a look that still melts me today. It all clicked. Over the next few days, we spent some time together. We both experienced that spark, that connection, that initial interest that led us to want to be with each other for as long as possible. Of course, we didn't know that we would spend the next thirty-plus years together.

Jodie: So, what was that exactly?
Reggie: Well, I think you can call it whatever you want, but I call it love.
Jodie: Aw, you're such a romantic.
Reggie: One of us has to be.
Jodie: [laughs] True. Better you than me!
Reggie: I think there's that attraction early on that makes people go, *Whoa! I've gotta get to know them!* Sometimes that grows into something more, but sometimes it doesn't. In our case, that initial attraction was very strong.
Jodie: Yeah, and we both trusted that feeling and didn't need a ton of time to know that it was something we needed to explore further.
Reggie: I think that's where love lives. You gotta be able to look at the person across from you and think, "I gotta figure out a way to get a little bit closer to that person each and every day." That feeling, that desire, can be a great fundamental building block.
Jodie: But can that initial desire be enough to sustain you forever and ever?

Reggie: Well, I don't know if it always can. It's worked for us so far, and it definitely helps when you have that initial spark.

Jodie: So the *real* question is: How do you turn that spark into a flame that is sustainable for years?

Growing up in Miami, I spent plenty of wild nights on the dance floor, but the night I met Reggie was different. The chemistry between us was unlike anything I'd ever felt. After rolling silverware at O'Charley's, a group of us went out dancing. We danced until the harsh lights of closing time forced us to separate. We hugged goodbye. Elated and forlorn, I left the club with my friend Monya and walked to her car. As I opened the car door, Reggie came running toward me, calling my name. Then he jumped on the back of the car, leaned over, and kissed me. Sparks flew even stronger than on the dance floor. I couldn't sleep that night, knowing that I was leaving to go back to Miami the next day. I didn't know how we could possibly make this work, but I also knew I would have to find a way.

I was 17 years old and a rising senior in high school. After I met Reggie, it felt like I had no choice—like I had to be with him... somehow. Little did I know that not only would I find a way for us to be together, but I would practically move heaven and earth to do so.

Jodie: Sometimes, I still find it hard to believe that two kids from totally different backgrounds just "happened" to meet over a forty-eight-hour window and found their way to a lifetime of love.

Reggie: It's easy to see now how we fueled that initial

spark into a flame. But at that time, we were simply following our hearts.

Jodie: Not our heads.

Reggie: The logical thing was that we'd *never* be able to make this work.

Jodie: There were way too many obstacles, from the physical distance to our age difference—

Reggie: To the color of our skin.

Jodie: But we didn't focus on any of that. Instead, we focused on how we felt about each other.

PHONE CALLS AND LETTERS

In the summer of 1990, long-distance communication wasn't easy. Reggie lived in Pensacola, and Jodie lived in Miami, so they couldn't see each other in person on a regular basis. There was no such thing as social media or iPhones. They didn't even have personal computers. The only way to communicate was to write letters or to talk on the phone—in Jodie's case, a single landline an entire family had to share. There was little privacy when it came to phone calls and verbal communication.

They wrote to each other almost daily about anything and everything—from the mundane activities of what they had for lunch to their mystical hopes and dreams. But letter writing, as meaningful as it was, offered little in the way of instant gratification. They *needed* to talk to each other, so to scratch that itch, they spent hours on the phone.

I still lived at home, and my family shared one phone. I couldn't possibly let the phone ring past 10:00 p.m. and wake the whole house, so Reggie and I created a system. We'd agree on a set time, and Reggie would call my house because he was the one paying—my parents would never spend hundreds of dollars on long-distance phone calls each month. At the agreed time, I would call a random number to occupy the line, and when Reggie called the houseline, I would be alerted via the call waiting signal.

That slow Southern drawl would greet me from miles away. I'd melt a little as a smile spread across my face. Then we'd talk for hours late into the night.

Because Jodie and Reggie could not see each other, their relationship evolved in unexpected ways. Reggie believes that their physical chemistry would have blinded them, and the physical distance allowed for a deeper, more meaningful, and intimate relationship than if they had lived in the same town. Through late-night talks and endless pages of letter writing, they learned so much about each other. They divulged their likes, dislikes, and what they valued most in relationships and in life. They spent hours and pages exploring each other's past and imagining their future. Those late-night talks and letters created safe and open communication. They discovered a level of unparalleled trust and deep companionship. Without realizing it, they were building a solid foundation—one that would sustain them for a lifetime—all from that initial spark.

During that first year, Reggie and Jodie had only seen each other a handful of times. Reggie was still stationed in Pensacola, so he would sneak down to Miami a few times. Jodie's parents didn't know he was coming to town. They knew about Reggie, but they thought of him as more of a pen pal than the love of Jodie's life.

When the talk of their relationship first came up, Jodie's parents were quick to try and nip it in the bud. After all, she was still in high school, and he was fully employed as an officer in the Navy. But they weren't going to stop talking or dating just because Jodie's parents weren't too keen on their relationship. Along the way, Jodie decided it was best to keep their relationship on the down-low. What her parents didn't know couldn't hurt them, right?

Jodie: During our first few years, nobody knew that we were a couple.
Reggie: Hell, they didn't even know we existed in each other's world.
Jodie: Yeah, there wasn't Instagram where we could post our rendezvous. Plus, our six-year age difference, and being an interracial couple, would appear to be insurmountable obstacles to others.
Reggie: Let's be real. The life experiences between eighteen and twenty-four could be vast—it's an important time of personal growth and independence.
Jodie: It is, but we never thought much about our age difference.
Reggie: I did!
Jodie: [laughs] Well, I didn't. And so our relationship grew in secret. It was just us. I really liked it that way... it was a lot easier.
Reggie: Yeah, no one really knew about us. Your parents didn't necessarily approve or disapprove of me. They knew

of me, but they didn't have the full information. Same with my parents. But we weren't dependent on any of them, which was a good thing.

Jodie: You certainly weren't. You were off adulting, but I was finishing high school and starting college and my parents were very much a part of my life. I valued their opinions greatly.

Reggie: True. And the reality of being an interracial couple and how the outside world viewed us was a whole 'nother piece of the puzzle.

Jodie: When our relationship was just us, we didn't have to deal with other people's judgment. Like I said, it was easier!

Reggie: But as we started letting more people in and they became aware of the depth of our relationship, their biases came to light, and it was something we had to face.

In the spring of 1991, Reggie and I had been in a committed relationship for many months. I was about to graduate high school, and I wanted to invite him to my senior prom. He was the only person I wanted to take to my prom, and I couldn't imagine going without him. Plus, all my friends heard me talk about him throughout our senior year and were dying to meet him. I asked him, and he said yes.

Then came the challenging part. I had to ask my parents if he could come, which meant telling them more about him. I knew I didn't want to freak them out, so I didn't tell them that I was madly in love with him. Instead, I tried to play it cool and shared with them how much I liked him, what a great guy he was, and how much I wanted him to come to my prom with me.

It was a difficult conversation—I had never done anything like this. Up until this point, I was their most stress-free child. I had only ever done what they said and acted according to their rules and expectations. But now, I was unexpectedly flipping the script. I was asking them if I could bring a fully grown 24-year-old man, who they'd never met, to my high school prom. Plus, did I mention that he's black?

My parents were totally taken aback and didn't know what to do, so they asked the teachers and nuns at my school to make the final decision. As you can imagine, it didn't take long for the faculty to deliberate. We were flat-out denied. The sad truth was that Reggie embodied everything that wasn't acceptable as a prom date—too different, too old, too independent, too "Black." He was just "too much" for a senior prom date at an all-girls Catholic high school.

Reggie: Yeah, that was a rough one. You were what people considered the "golden girl." You got good grades. You were a cheerleader. You were a student body officer. Everyone liked you and wanted you on their team. You followed the rules and set examples.
Jodie: Eh, pretty much.
Reggie: So it was kinda a big deal when you boycotted the prom.
Jodie: It totally was! It was also the only stance I knew how to take—the little bit of activism, as small as it was.
Reggie: You sent a message, though. They never thought you wouldn't go. They thought you'd accept their decision and just conform to what they believed was best for you.
Jodie: That was the first time it became clear to me that the people I looked up to and who claimed to care about me weren't actually interested in how I felt or what I knew

to be true. They decided they knew better and refused to trust my judgment.

Reggie: It's interesting because this gets to the start of us truly realizing what we felt for each other and also understanding that the rest of the world definitely didn't see us the way we saw ourselves.

Jodie: I do feel that this created a deeper connection for us and gave us a little taste of what we were gonna face in the years to come—hints of people who thought they knew better and didn't think that we should be together.

Reggie: They didn't see the brightness and love that we saw in our relationship. They all seemed to focus on the worst-case scenario: He's older and more worldly, so he *must* be trying to take advantage of you. Plus, he's Black.

Jodie: But despite all that, we always came back to us and our path. We had the conviction and belief in who we were and what we were feeling.

Reggie: We did. But it was really tough for you when your support system—the people you always turned to for guidance and advice, helping you to navigate life's path—betrayed you. It was an eye-opening experience for you. I'd been through this type of situation before. I was used to being let down by those I trusted and looked to for guidance.

―――

I still remember my first experience growing up in Macon, Georgia, when I realized that my heroes did not necessarily think or see the world like I did. To me, the world was pretty black and white. I didn't have the experience yet to realize that we are swimming in a sea of gray. The good thing about being naive is that you're very confident in your beliefs. To say I was a very opinionated young man would be an understatement. I had very strong opinions and beliefs. Growing up, I had many interesting discussions with my mom. She had a tough time convincing her strong-willed teenager that I didn't know as much in my thirteen years as she did in her thirty-plus years.

One time, my mom and I got into a heated discussion about what I should do if I ever got a girl I was dating pregnant. My mom made it very clear that the only course of action was to marry the girl. Man, it got hot when I told her I would only marry the girl if I loved her. I would take responsibility for both her and the child, but getting married may not be the right call. I believed any relationship that is built on a foundation that is anything other than love is doomed to fail, and the ramifications for that failure would be much worse than anything else. I was determined to only marry for love. In the end, as is so often the case, the universe worked it all out for me. When Jodie and I discovered that we were pregnant, we decided to get married as my mother would have wanted. Fortunately for me, I also got what I wanted because I was marrying the love of my life.

WESTWARD BOUND

In the summer of 1991, shortly after being together for a year, the Navy stationed Reggie on the other side of the country in California. Jodie went off to college at the University of Florida. Getting together in person meant that one of them would have to fly across the country. Jodie had moved out of her parents' house but was not completely free from their rules, so in order to see Reggie, she'd have to make that trip without their knowing. This began the era of their cross-country rendezvous.

I'd hop on a red-eye flight in Florida wearing sweats, an oversized tee, and tennis shoes. I'd spend the first few hours trying to sleep, but I was always too excited. Shortly before the plane landed, I'd head to the bathroom and change into a cute little dress, slip on a pair of pumps, and put on makeup. Butterflies danced in my stomach in anticipation of seeing Reggie. I was so excited to see him but also slightly nervous, wondering if this would be the time the spark died or if something had changed between us. But it never did.

Reggie would greet me at the baggage claim. He always looked super cute, wearing Obsession for Men cologne, holding fresh flowers, or a thoughtful gift. There were always those first awkward moments of seeing each other again after so many months apart, but once we started talking, everything felt right and normal again.

Those weekends they spent together were so precious. Though the days would fly by, they had such a rush of excitement and adrenaline, and the thrill of seeing each other never dulled. Every time they parted, they never knew when they would see each other again, so saying goodbye was bittersweet. After getting their "fix" over a long weekend, they'd go through withdrawals until they could be together again. Those wild rendezvous weekends, followed by long months of separation, allowed them to cocoon into each other, preparing them for the obstacles that were looming just over the horizon.

Jodie: Actually, I'm pretty sure that first night at O'Charley's, while you were still in the thralls of love at first sight, you asked me to marry you.
Reggie: I might have.
Jodie: You definitely invited me to move to California with you.
Reggie: That would've worked for me. I remember when we first started dating, you said I don't want to wait, let's just get married, and I'll figure out college as we go.
Jodie: I did. I was pretty clear about that early on, but you were pretty set on sticking to the plan, which involved me going to college, getting my degree, and *then* getting married.
Reggie: I like to make plans and stick to them.
Jodie: You really do. But college wasn't my highest priority. I knew I could figure that out. My highest priority was us. Apparently, I was manifesting what I really wanted since the day we met.
Reggie: If you had told me more about all this manifestation stuff that you talk about now, we might have seen it coming.
Jodie: True! We would have realized that another plan was actually coming together—one we had set into motion behind the scenes without even knowing it. So we wouldn't have been so surprised that after one of our secret rendezvouses, we found ourselves unexpectedly pregnant.
Reggie: Hey, you can't be giving away the story!

In the spring of 1992, I was traveling to California to see Reggie. Our last secret rendezvous had been six weeks prior—and I was late. The kind of late an 18-year-old college co-ed doesn't want to be. I was super stressed about it, but I wanted to wait to take a pregnancy test until we were together.

The first thing I did when I got to Reggie's apartment was race to the bathroom. He had bought a pregnancy test for me, so I peed on the stick and placed it on the counter. We sat on the cool tile floor in his tiny bathroom—time seemed to stand still. When the two-minute timer finally went off, I asked him to look first—he's brave like that. He stood up, read the results, then held out his hand and helped me stand up. The test came back positive. We held each other, our bodies swaying, slow dancing right there in that tiny bathroom. There was no music, but we didn't need any. No words were spoken, but we didn't need any of those either. In that moment, everything had changed, and all we needed was each other.

Jodie: There was never a doubt between us. It was just so easy to know our next steps.
Reggie: Yep, your plan to entrap me finally worked.
Jodie: Ha-ha, very funny. I'm pretty sure it was your attempt to entrap *me*.
Reggie: [laughs] Well, it worked! I remember telling you that you didn't have to keep the baby if it was too much. If that wasn't the road you wanted to go down, I'd make it work. I would raise the child on my own with the help of my mother and the rest of my family. I knew exactly what I wanted, which was for us to have our baby and build a life together, but I always wanted you to be sure.
Jodie: I never felt any pressure from you, one way or the

other. I also knew exactly what I wanted to do. I never had any doubts. I wanted to get married and start our family way earlier than planned.

Reggie: Giddyup! Here we go!

Jodie: The challenging part was that our relationship was now going to be exposed to other people's influence and opinions. I recall lots of "well-meaning" people voicing their concern, not about you and me—a black man and a white woman—getting married but rather our children.

Reggie: Is "well-meaning" people code for "racist"?

Jodie: [laughs] Pretty much! But these people were really insistent and questioned me as to how our children (being biracial) would survive in this world. They wanted to be sure that I was actively considering this.

Reggie: So they were just trying to make it all about our children? Their real objection to us being together was conveniently placed on the well-being of our kids?

Jodie: Correct. This objection never made any sense to me.

Reggie: Obviously.

Jodie: [Ha!] I would simply respond that our children would be raised with love. Period. And that a loving household, no matter what it looked like, was the most important thing for any child and their well-being.

Reggie: Did it shut them up?

Jodie: Not always. But my focus wasn't on them or the rest of the world. I figured we would just show them rather than try to explain anything more. Plus, my focus was on us, our baby, and our family.

Reggie: Yes, well, we also knew that once a child was involved, things would shift with our families, too. It's a total game-changer. Both of our parents weren't going to be outside looking in. They were going to want to be involved with their grandchild's upbringing.

Jodie: Plus, we knew we wanted them to be a part of their grandchild's life, too—that was important to both of us.

Reggie: I felt an additional challenge about us getting married while you were still so young. I was concerned that you would feel robbed one day because you didn't go to your prom or have a typical college experience or have other wild and crazy times because of our relationship.

Jodie: I always found it interesting that this was such a concern of yours because it was never really a concern of mine.

Reggie: I mean, it's true... you've never been a really wild partier. But you did have your moments, like that trip to Mexico and entering bikini contests.

Jodie: I did do that, but when it comes down to it, I'm just an old soul.

Reggie: An old soul who enters bikini contests?

Jodie: [laughing] C'mon, I grew up in Miami! Bikinis are a complete ensemble there. The truth is, I went clubbing and dancing long before I went to college, and I did it in Miami Beach—not a lot of other places can compare to that. I didn't need to do a lot of partying and experimenting in college. Plus, I knew exactly what I wanted, and that was you.

―――

FINAL THOUGHTS

Was it love at first sight? Reggie and Jodie would have to say yes! But the more compelling part of their story was how they turned that initial spark into a sustainable flame that has been burning for over three decades. They still marvel at how they transformed their powerful connection into a strong and beautiful relationship.

The key element in strengthening the foundation of any relationship is trust—not only trusting in your partner but, more importantly, trusting yourself. Jodie and Reggie trusted how they felt about each other and knew what was best for them. They had confidence that they could make the best decisions both as individuals and as a couple. They trusted that their love would carry them through whatever came their way.

Most of the work necessary to ensure that the initial spark grows into a robust flame and is sustainable comes from within. Both you and your partner need to do your own internal work to actively support the continued growth and success of the relationship. While your paths for personal growth may be wildly different, each person must take their own journey. Through your own growth process, you can create more grace and space for not only yourself but for your partner.

When they discovered they were pregnant, they came together on the same page. They made decisions individually and as a couple long before anyone else's advice, opinions, or guidance could influence them in any way.

This became the key to the foundation of "them" as a couple—something they learned very early on and have returned to time and again over the course of their relationship. Throughout the years, they focused on their needs first, even if that meant shutting out the rest of the world.

KEY TAKEAWAY

Trusting yourself and following your heart creates a beautiful relationship journey. When you remain firm in your beliefs and feelings for each other, your relationship will be rooted in love and ensure that love at first sight lasts a lifetime.

WHAT THEY WISH THEY HAD KNOWN: MOON SIGN

A long-standing question (joking or not) at the start of any relationship is, "What's your sign?" And while knowing your partner's astrological Sun sign is both fun and useful, understanding their astrological Moon sign can be even more significant.

Your Sun sign represents the brighter, outward parts of you. Your Moon sign represents your innermost self. It provides insights into your most basic emotional needs. It is often said that your Moon sign represents the "real" you. Your Moon sign reflects *how* you process emotions and alerts you to what makes you *feel* safe and secure. Understanding your own Moon sign provides deep insights into how to best nurture your inner self. Taking care to satisfy your Moon sign is tantamount to learning healthy coping strategies and emotional regulation.

When you understand your *partner's* Moon sign, it is a total relationship game changer. This knowledge is valuable insider information! It offers an intimate window into your partner's inner self. When you understand your partner's Moon sign, you can begin to understand what makes *them* feel safe, regulated, and fulfilled at an instinctual level.

Reggie is a Gemini Moon, and like all Gemini Moons, his innermost self is mercurial and highly energetic. He is quick, playful, and highly curious. He thrives on continual mental stimulation and intellectual engagement. Jodie is a Libra Moon, and like all Libra Moons, she values beauty, balance, and harmony above all. She feels fulfilled when bringing people together and contributing to peace on all levels. She thrives in meaningful connection and partnership.

Furthermore, both of their Moons (Gemini and Libra) are Air signs. Air signs share a love of open communication and have a desire to explore ideas freely. This informs us that Jodie and Reggie not only enjoy stimulating conversations, but that their lively banter is fulfilling at an emotional level and helps to ensure that they both feel safe and connected. This gives deeper insights into how and why their relationship was built on letter writing and late-night phone calls. It also explains why Reggie and Jodie decided to launch a podcast. Storytelling is deeply satisfying to both Gemini and Libra Moons and simply put, when your Moon (i.e., your innermost self) is satisfied, then your *entire* being is satisfied.

On the other hand, when it comes to emotional connection, Reggie's Gemini Moon prefers to always keep it light-hearted and would rather avoid deep emotional conversations, while Jodie's Libra Moon craves and requires deeper emotional connection with her partner to feel safe.

In real-life application, learning about Reggie's Gemini Moon and its inherent desire to always be mentally stimulated helped Jodie understand why Reggie was *always* playing games like chess, sudoku, hearts, or spades. Even when they were watching a movie or spending quality time together, Reggie was playing any number of games on his phone.

For years, Jodie misread this as disinterest. She erroneously took it as a sign that Reggie would rather be elsewhere and her internal Libra Moon self, which values meaningful connection above all, would feel hurt and rejected. But when she learned about his Gemini Moon, Jodie began to understand that his nightly game playing was simply a form of self-soothing at the end of a long day and that keeping his mind active was essential to his winding down so that he *could* enjoy their quality time together.

Over the years, the basic differences in how their innermost selves prefer to communicate, connect, and ultimately feel safe have become a growth opportunity for the couple. Having known about each other's Moon signs from the start of their relationship would have alleviated many frustrations and misunderstandings and allowed them to support each other at a deeper emotional level even sooner.

To learn more about Moon signs, natal astrology, and how it informs their relationship, watch this exclusive live clip with Jodie and Reggie!

SCAN THE QR CODE:

GUESS WHO'S COMING TO DINNER?

After Jodie and Reggie discovered they were pregnant, they created a beautiful plan for their future together. Jodie was going to finish her freshman year of college and then move to California. They were going to get married, have their baby, and live... happily ever after.

However, there was one obstacle in their way. They'd been together for almost two years, but Reggie still hadn't met Jodie's parents. Heck, they barely even knew that he was part of her life. This meeting was one for the ages.

Finding a window of time for this meeting before they planned to get married was complicated. At the time, Reggie was living and working near San Francisco, while Jodie's parents lived in Miami. Jodie only had a few weeks left of her freshman year at the University of Florida, and once she completed it, she planned to move across the country to be with Reggie.

By chance, Reggie had been relocated for a month to Key West, Florida, to fly missions in support of counter-drug operations in Latin America. Now that everyone was in Florida, Jodie drove home for the weekend so this meeting could finally happen.

Jodie: I was crazy anxious about you meeting my parents for the first time. And all you could say was...
Reggie: They're gonna love me!
Jodie: "They're gonna love me!" You said that over and over and over! You drove me crazy with that. Oh, and your other favorite saying was, "It's going to be fine."
Reggie: I said that because it was true. Parents always love me, and it *was* going to be just fine.
Jodie: Other parents might love you, but you'd never met someone's parents for the first time to tell them that you planned to marry their nineteen-year-old pregnant daughter and move her to the other side of the country.
Reggie: True, true. Still, I had no doubt they were going to love me.
Jodie: As charming as you were, I still wasn't convinced my parents would like you. In fact, I was quite certain it was NOT going to be love at first sight.

If there is one example of the level of confidence and hubris I had at twenty-four, meeting Jodie's parents for the first time was it. They had barely even heard about me. The only question they ever had to answer about me was, "Can he come to prom?" And the answer was a solid "No" by home, church, and school. I was about to stroll into their living room and introduce myself after knocking up their precious, perfect baby girl.

Part of my confidence in this very awkward situation stemmed from the fact that I wasn't coming with my hat in hand to ask for their permission to marry Jodie. I was in a financial position to support us. I had everything in place to make our lives work, so I didn't need anything from them. Jodie and I had already decided on our plan. I was planning to tell them how I intended to take care of their beautiful girl. The way I saw it, the choice was theirs: We could either be nice and polite to each other, and all move forward together, or they could be assholes, in which case Jodie and I would move on without them.

To her entire family's credit, it went as well as anyone could hope. Jodie and her brother, Todd, picked me up from the base in Key West. The ride to Miami couldn't have been more open and friendly, at least for me and Todd. Jodie was horribly anxious, but Todd and I were joking and relaxed. Having him around really helped diffuse some of the tension. After the initial introductions and pleasantries, Jodie's dad asked me to join him on the back porch. He wanted to have a man-to-man discussion. Her dad did what I was hoping he would do: He gave me a chance. Once he realized the amount of love and commitment I had for his daughter, he became much more accepting of me. At the time, I thought it went so well because "I" was so easy to love, but now I realize that it went well because of how much they loved Jodie.

Jodie: That was an intense weekend, but maybe we should backtrack to a few weekends before when I had to tell them, all by myself, that I was pregnant.

Reggie: [laughs] You mean that weekend when your mom canceled Easter?

Jodie: [laughs] Yes, that one. My mom was ahead of her time—she created cancel culture in the spring of 1992.

Reggie: Wasn't that when she told the rest of your fam that you weren't having Easter?
Jodie: To be precise, she bluntly told them, "Your sister is pregnant! Easter is canceled!"

It was the spring of 1992, and my roommate and bestie, Susie, drove me home on Easter weekend. I was nineteen years old and in my freshman year of college. That five-hour drive from Gainesville to Miami was the longest of my life. I felt like I was going to vomit the entire ride, not because I was pregnant, but because I was terrified. Reggie and I were ready to begin our lives together, and I was about to tell my parents that I was pregnant, dropping out of the University of Florida, getting married to a man they'd never met, and I was moving to California in four weeks.

It was the hardest conversation of my life. My parents loved me, but I didn't know how they would respond. I'd already had a few weeks to get used to the news, but I was still in shock. I knew it was going to be a huge, unexpected blow for my parents, and it would be A LOT for them to take in.

I decided to wait for my dad to get home from work so I could tell them together. Plus, I knew I wouldn't be able to say it more than once. The sun was setting when I finally mustered up the courage. I sat them down on the couch in the family room. Wringing my hands and feeling like I was about to throw up, I just spit it all out.

My mom started yelling. She wasn't yelling so much at me as she was at the situation. I had expected as much. Then she said that she needed some air, so she grabbed her car keys and left the house. My dad was very quiet. He stood up and walked out through the glass sliding doors of the family room onto the back porch. He'd left the door open, allowing the humid Florida night air to creep into the house. I sat frozen on my spot on the couch. I couldn't move. I didn't know what to do. I had spent so much energy thinking about this conversation, but I hadn't thought much beyond it. After a few minutes, my dad walked back into the house. Without saying a word, he opened his arms to me, and I ran to him. He held me tightly as I cried and cried.

NEW LIFE IN CALIFORNIA

Within a few short months, everything Jodie and Reggie had dreamed about came to pass. They were finally going to create the life they had envisioned together. The hardest part was telling Jodie's parents, but all things considered, they had taken the news rather well. Now, as parents themselves, Jodie and Reggie appreciate how challenging that must have been for her parents. Through all the upheaval, unexpected news, and heartbreak, her parents did their best to focus on how much they loved their daughter and supported her, even when they weren't sure if she was making the "right" decision.

For two years, Jodie had kept her parents in the dark about Reggie. It became a lot easier to simply exclude them from this aspect of her life, as she reasoned there would be less resistance this way. But after she told them about her pregnancy, she had no choice but to lay all her cards out. She began to share more with her parents, giving them the complete picture so they could begin to understand the depth of her love for Reggie. Being honest helped shift her parents' perspective, and they realized how committed the couple was to each other. As soon as Jodie completed her one and only year at the University of Florida, she packed up her suitcases, flew to California to start a new life, and never looked back.

GUESS WHO'S COMING TO DINNER?

Jodie: It's kinda hard to believe that my entire life fit into two suitcases.
Reggie: I'm pretty sure today's Jodie can't even go on a trip to California with only two suitcases, much less move her entire life somewhere.
Jodie: And the problem with that is...?
Reggie: [laughs] Nothing, nothing at all.
Jodie: [laughs] That's what I thought. Once I got to California, we had a quickie shotgun wedding at the Santa Clara County Courthouse.
Reggie: And the bride wore white.
Jodie: Yes, I did. Again, was there a problem with this?
Reggie: [still laughing] No, none at all. You were beautiful.
Jodie: Thank you.
Reggie: The other part of our plan was to have a full-blown wedding on our first anniversary in May 1993.
Jodie: Once you were back from your first Navy deployment, and I could fit into my dream wedding dress.
Reggie: But before all that, we had to figure out how to actually live with each other.

Reggie and I went from seeing each other only a few times a year to living in a tiny apartment together. Living together was actually better than I expected. I think we both dreamed about it for so long, and that dream carried us through much of that initial transition time. For me, the bigger challenge was that I had zero understanding of "Navy life." I was completely clueless. For anyone unfamiliar with military life, it is its own unique world—with rules and customs and jargon and tradi-

tions that were totally foreign to me. I didn't know an ensign from an admiral, an officer from an enlisted, a squadron from a cavalry. Between the Navy, being a new wife, being pregnant for the first time, and being an East Coast girl living on the West Coast, I was on a short learning curve.

The most unexpected part of all this "newness" in my life was the sisterhood of women I'd met during those first years of marriage. They were other Navy spouses, many of whom were also newlyweds, pregnant for the first time, or just starting their families. We were all figuring out "Navy life" together. These women took me in. We leaned on each other and started to grow together. These friendships set the tone for camaraderie and sisterhood over the next twenty-eight years of my life in the Navy and beyond. I learned how to mother, how to survive with Reggie being gone and adjust to life when he came home, how to move my family alone, and so much more. The support of these women, as I witnessed them navigate marriage and motherhood while living this Navy life, increased my confidence in my own mothering abilities as a young wife. To this day, these same women are my "ride or dies."

NEWLYWEDS PUT TO THE TEST

The foundation of their marriage was tested very quickly. Reggie and Jodie had only about five months of living together and seeing each other every day before they became parents. Then, just a few weeks after they welcomed their beautiful baby girl, Olivia, into the world, Reggie was deployed for the first time. He was scheduled to be gone for the next six months. Jodie was going to have to face postpartum and all the newborn firsts without him.

In 1992, social media, laptops, cell phones, and Facetime did not exist. To stay connected during Reggie's first deployment, they returned to the form of communication they had perfected when dating: letter writing. An important element in any lasting relationship is to find something that works and come back to it. The process or the experience might look a little different, but if it worked before, it's worth trying it again.

Thus began the next era of letter writing. While these letters still spoke of wanting to be together, Jodie's letters were also filled with details of life as a new mother. Reggie's letters spoke more about what a typical twenty-five-year-old man would be concerned with. Their letters have stood the test of time, and all these years later, Jodie and Reggie still revisit them. Whenever they have a weekend getaway, they grab a random handful of their old letters and read them to each other.

Jodie: My letters were about a crying baby or being up all night, teething and nursing, while yours talked about how much you missed me and how you couldn't wait to get into my pants again.

Reggie: Ha! It's very entertaining to read them now. And not much has changed!

Jodie: At the time, it was oddly reassuring to know that you were still attracted to me even after I had a baby. I remember thinking, *He hasn't seen me lately, so he doesn't actually know what I look like or feel like right now.*

Reggie: But that didn't matter.

Jodie: Your letters reassured me in ways I didn't realize I needed, all the way from the other side of the world.

Reggie: Our letters were really such a foundational part of our communication, and we could be honest about how we felt. It always brought our focus back to us, especially during the challenging times ahead.

At that time, the challenge for me was figuring out how to balance being a new husband and father and still perform at the highest possible level in my Navy squadron. The Navy is an up-or-out organization, which creates a constant Highlander *situation. In the movie, there can be only one at the end of the competition. In a Navy command, everyone is rated against each other, and there can be only one top-ranked individual. If you're not the best or close to it, your opportunities are very limited to advance in a naval career and get the best orders. I was in a very competitive environment while also trying to figure out how to give my new family everything they needed from me as far as time and attention. I had to figure it all out on the fly: how to* be a successful naval officer, how to be a supportive, loving husband, and how to be a great dad.

The bright spot for me was that I was living my dream. I always wanted a fun, exciting career, but more than that, I always wanted a family. This motivated and excited me as I tried to figure out how to meet these challenges. It became a daily trial-and-error process, with communication and discussion with Jodie as the cornerstone. The key piece to making it all work was prioritizing my relationship, which would ensure that the other two areas were taken care of. I constantly asked myself: How can I make this easier for her? How can I make this work? How can I make her see that she's supported? How can I make her feel the love I have for her?

Over time, I found it was great to ask these questions, but the key to successfully answering them was to simply *ask her* instead of trying to guess what made her happy. It was one of those times when I wish I knew then what I know now. The only person who can really make Jodie happy is Jodie. My job is to constantly vibe with her to figure out how I can support her.

This was another transitional time in our relationship. We were figuring out our roles as new parents and as a husband-and-wife team, while also deciding how the Navy would be prioritized in our lives. It allowed us to develop the guiding principles that we still follow today: Nothing is more important than our relationship, and family comes above all else. We make decisions together, so we have a united front. Putting those rules into action is not always an easy process. I wish I understood myself better back then because it would have helped me handle my frustrations. When the relationship starts to have multiple challenges and constant pulls, the key to "winning" is to always make sure your partner knows they are the most important thing in the world.

LEARNING HOW TO BECOME PARENTS

As any parent knows, when they are actually doing the parenting thing, it can be a whole different ball game. Many parents have theories and ideas about how they want to parent, but those are just great ideas until they are actually *doing* it.

The truth is that everyone shows up to the parenting gig equipped with the tools that their parents and caregivers used to raise them. You have a choice about which tools you plan to keep or discard. If you don't want to stick with something that has been passed down to you, feel free to ditch it. You are in the driver's seat and can decide which tools you want to add or keep in your parenting repertoire.

Discipline was one area where Jodie and Reggie had very different viewpoints. One of the biggest parenting discussions arose early on with the question of spanking. Today, the discussion about whether to spank your child might seem like an antiquated conversation, but in the early nineties, it was a hot parenting topic. Jodie and Reggie both grew up in households where spanking was part of the discipline.

> **Reggie:** Well, Jodie only got one spanking when she was little, and her dad cried more than her. So yeah, I guess you could say there was spanking in her household.
> **Jodie:** Wait, what? That wasn't *your* childhood experience, too? You got more than one spanking growing up?
> **Reggie**: Uh... yes.
> **Jodie:** Well, despite how I grew up, my philosophy on disciplining was clear: You don't need to spank to modify behavior.

Reggie: In my world, spanking had nothing to do with love. Spanking was accountability. You did something, and then you got a spanking. I never thought my parents loved me any less or didn't like me because I did something wrong. I simply got a spanking for it. And that worked for me. I mean, if you get hit the right way, you ain't doing that again. It modified behavior.
Jodie: Um, there's A LOT to unpack there.
Reggie: Maybe. You said, "There will be no spanking in our house."
Jodie: I believed there was zero need to spank our child to modify behavior or create accountability.
Reggie: After a lot of back and forth, we compromised. I said, "Okay, we'll raise the first kid your way, but if she turns out to be a little shit, we're spanking all the rest."
Jodie: I had no problem making that deal with you because, well, I knew I'd win. I knew we wouldn't need to spank any of our children. I also knew that she'd be an angel on top of it all.
Reggie: I had my doubts.
Jodie: I know. But that's why I agreed to it, because I knew that if it's what you needed to feel comfortable moving forward, then I had no problem agreeing to your "compromise."
Reggie: I think the key takeaway for me is that compromise piece. To this day, I can't think of many things that we've dug our heels in and said, "No, it's my way or it's no way." Everything has always been up for negotiation. In the case of spanking, though, you said yes, knowing that you were never going to let it go my way.
Jodie: Correct.
Reggie: But you at least made me think it might.

Jodie: I'm sweet like that sometimes.

———

Jodie and Reggie realized early on that compromise was an inherent part of their relationship and its success. If one of them is more passionate about or has a strong opinion about something, then they're willing to explore both sides of the equation. Even when they may not totally agree, they're always open to having the discussion and say, "I'm willing to step back a little and let you take the lead on this one." That's what Reggie did with the decision not to spank their children. They successfully navigated parenting without spanking their first child, who was a strong-willed angel, and they never spanked any of their other children either.

———

I don't know if you could have a better first child than Olivia. If there could be the personification of the love shared by two people, it would be that child. She was such a gift. She was the first grandchild for two grandmothers who loved nothing more than a girly girl to spoil. The dress didn't have enough frills. There was always room for one more dress, doll, or hair bow. Olivia loved being the center of attention, so it was a relationship made in heaven. When Olivia turned two, I helped Jodie clean out her closet to make room for all the new clothes she had received from her grandmothers and aunties. There were at least thirty outfits in her closet that still had tags on them. To be clear, Olivia never wore the same outfit twice.

———

GUESS WHO'S COMING TO DINNER?

When Olivia was born, the whole dynamic shifted, not just for Jodie and Reggie but for the extended family as well. Anyone who had been a little uncertain about this unexpected pregnancy became her biggest fan. She transformed everyone's life for the better. Any discord and disconnect seemed to dissolve. Reggie and Jodie were grateful and relieved that everyone agreed that having Olivia was a true blessing.

When my parents and in-laws came to town, I always did little things to see if they would share their opinions about how we were raising Miss Olivia. I wanted them to know that it was okay to share their opinions, but the final call would always be up to me and Jodie. One of my tests was how I would "hold" Olivia. I was a football player growing up, and one of my favorite things to do was run around the house with Olivia tucked in my arm like a football. It drove Jodie's mom crazy, but she never said a word about it. To their credit, my in-laws and my parents were very supportive of how we raised our kids, which allowed us to parent how we saw fit.

The bigger challenge was making sure the grandparents respected the boundaries that Jodie and I created. They loved Olivia so much and loved to give her anything and everything. We always presented a united front to our families about what was allowed and what wasn't. This united approach really ensured that we received the consistent behavior we wanted.

FINAL THOUGHTS

The first years of marriage taught Jodie and Reggie the value of compromise and how to always be open to each other's way of doing things, even if it wasn't their preferred method. To thrive as a couple, you need to give your partner space to try out things that interest them. It's important to be open and receptive to each other's ideas and interests.

Returning to what worked for Jodie and Reggie and their communication style was vital to the health of their relationship. Whether it was writing letters from across the world or middle-of-the-night phone calls, they kept the communication lines open. Once they discovered what worked, they prioritized it, even when it seemed silly or extra to others.

Trusting yourself and your partner before anything and everything is the name of the game. That foundation of trust will keep growing and strengthening amidst the challenges of the outside world. For Jodie and Reggie, the opposition of outsiders often strengthened their resolve and commitment to each other.

You can't make each other happy, nor is it your job to. Reggie spent many years attempting to make Jodie happy, but he was going about it all wrong. He was using the lens of what would make *him* happy and attempting to apply that to Jodie. It took some time to realize that it is up to each partner to do their own dive deep and discover what makes them truly happy.

Reggie and Jodie had decided that due to the inherently unstable nature of Navy life, one of them would become the primary caregiver. Jodie decided to take on this role of being the parent who provided consistency and stability. They weren't always sure how they would make it work, living off a single-family income, but they decided to give it a try.

Learning how to parent and realizing they could decide what

kind of family they wanted to create was a powerful awareness for both of them. While they allowed themselves to be informed by their parents' choices, they also realized that they didn't need to be limited by them. It often takes more effort to do things differently, and it doesn't always turn out exactly as imagined. But even at the young ages of nineteen and twenty-five, they understood the importance of forging their parenting path together.

KEY TAKEAWAY

Find a special way to connect (like letter writing) that works for your relationship and come back to it often. Through the years, the process or the experience might look a little different, but if it worked before, it's worth trying it again and will inevitably get your connection back on track or strengthen it further.

WHAT THEY WISH THEY HAD KNOWN: ENNEAGRAM

Personality typing systems like Myers Briggs or Clifton Strengths have long been used for personal discovery and team building. For Jodie and Reggie, there is one personality typing system that stands far above the rest in both personal development and relationship strengthening and that is Enneagram.

Enneagram is a numeric system that includes Types 1 through 9. Enneagram describes people in terms of their core motivations, desires, and most basic fears. It is based on ancient spiritual traditions and helps individuals understand their primary driver in life, whether it be peace, connection, or security.

When people understand their Enneagram Type, they can begin to understand *why they do the things they do.* And in turn, when someone understands their partner's Enneagram, they can begin to understand *why their partner does the things they do-* which, let's face it, can often be a complete mystery! Enneagram unveils that mystery and brings clarity to how we (and our partner) perceive the world around us. It also exposes the root of our core emotions- particularly during times of stress. Enneagram sheds a tender light on one's greatest fears—such as being insignificant and feeling worthless (Type 3) or experiencing loss, disconnection, and disharmony (Type 9).

Reggie is an Enneagram Type 3, "The Overachiever," while Jodie is an Enneagram Type 9, "The Peacemaker." While both types deeply value connection and relationships, they express it differently.

- Jodie: (Type 9) prefers peace and harmony above all—especially in relationships.
- Reggie: (Type 3) desires validation and admiration.

One of the challenges that can surface between these Enneagram types is in how they deal with conflict.

- Jodie: (Type 9) prefers to avoid conflict *all* together and strives to maintain peace.
- Reggie: (Type 3) prefers to attack conflict head-on with direct communication and immediate action.

On the other hand, there are powerful benefits to these types in relationships.

- Jodie: (Type 9) will bring harmony, focus, grounding, and stability to Reggie's (Type 3) constant striving, always moving forward, and ever-ambitious nature.
- Jodie: (Type 9) also helps Reggie's (Type 3) be more present, gently reminding him the value of living in the here and now rather than always striving toward the future.
- Reggie: (Type 3) motivates Jodie's (Type 9) hesitancy to take action, do the thing, and step out of her comfort zone. He emboldens her to actively achieve her dreams.

The gift of Enneagram is that it allows us to understand our own motivations, emotions, and fears so that we can then show up in our relationships with more compassion, less judgment, more understanding, and greater empathy. When we are able to show up in relationships as *our* authentic selves, we are then able to see and accept our partner as *their* authentic selves, creating a powerful bond of unity and growth.

Learn more about Enneagram and how it has informed Jodie and Reggie's relationship by listening to: Episode 20: The Enneagram Episode of *Higher Love: The Podcast.*
SCAN THE QR CODE:

OUR ROARING TWENTIES

Jodie: Our twenties looked *a little* different from what our grown children's twenties have been like.

Reggie: Well, the first half of my twenties was pretty consistent with the rest of the world, but the second half of my twenties, and the entire twenties decade for you, was different from most.

Jodie: [laughing] Yep, I feel like my twenties were what most people's thirties look like.

Reggie: By the time you hit thirty, we'd been married for over a decade and had three kids.

Jodie: True. But I did have at least one typical twenties experience: I had a college experience.

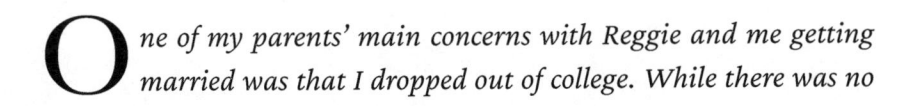

One of my parents' main concerns with Reggie and me getting married was that I dropped out of college. While there was no way I could continue going to school at the University of Florida, they wanted me to promise that I would find a way to get my degree. Reggie was also adamant about this. To be honest, getting a degree didn't mean that much to me one way or the other, but it sure meant a lot to the people I loved, so I enrolled at a community college once I got settled in California. It was really tricky, though, because we had to move every few years without knowing where the Navy would relocate us. This was long before online classes were even an option.

After I had Olivia, the Navy moved us from California to Washington State, so I found another community college where I continued taking classes. Little by little, I made my way, inching toward my degree. I felt a lot more invested in my education because I was taking it slowly, and we were paying for it ourselves. I actually took classes I wanted to take instead of those I thought I "should" take. I majored in English Literature and minored in Art History because those subjects brought me the most joy. After having a child and spending most of my days with a toddler, I actually looked forward to going to class in the evening, talking with adults, and writing papers.

Jodie: In the summer of 1997, I completed my bachelor's degree. It only took me six years, four colleges, two cross-country moves, and two kids—mostly while you were gone on multiple deployments and detachments—but I finally got it done.

Reggie: Come on, you graduated magna cum laude, summa cum laude... Which one of those lattes did you graduate with? What is the highest one again?

Jodie: [laughs] Summa cum laude is the highest "latte" there is.

Reggie: Then that's the one you got.

Jodie: Correct.
Reggie: And why was that?
Jodie: Why?
Reggie: Because I told you from the very beginning, "If you bring home anything less than an A, I'm cutting you off."
Jodie: [laughs] Yeah, *that* was why I got all A's throughout my entire college career!
Reggie: Well, you also graduated faster than your big brother, and he's two years older than you.
Jodie: That's not exactly true. He finished before me—just barely, but he did.
Reggie: You still kind of had a legit college experience. In a naval aviation squadron with lots of young junior officers, there's plenty of partying going on. We were surrounded by professional college partiers.
Jodie: [Hmph] There is only so much partying you can do when you have to get up with a baby the next morning.
Reggie: Yeah, I've never had to get up with a baby, so I don't know what that's all about.
Jodie: [Ha-ha!] But seriously, I didn't miss college life. My first year at the University of Florida was plenty enough for me.
Reggie: But the Navy gave you the college experience you "missed"—the friends, the partying… you got it all through the Navy.
Jodie: Yup, whether I wanted it or not, the Navy gave it to me!

———

While in the squadron, I struggled to be one of "the boys" while also being there as much as possible for my family. One time, I set up a huge party for the squadron to blow off some steam after working 24/7 for a few weeks. My squadron mates loved boating out on the water in Jacksonville, so I organized a huge "boatex."[i] We had a pontoon boat with a grill and music, which served as the main hub where all the other boats would tie up. We were water skiing and partying like rock stars. As the party started to rage, I realized it was time for me to leave because I had promised Jodie I would be home at a certain time. I wanted to stay, but I had made the mistake too many times of telling Jodie one thing but doing another, and I didn't want to make that mistake again. From my past missteps, I learned one key thing that eased the conflict between the dueling priorities of home and work: Jodie didn't care what I did as long as I did what I said I was going to do. So I happily got a ride to shore, jumped into my car, and took my ass home. I always enjoyed hanging out with the boys, but it never compared to the joy of being home with my family.

Reggie: I think our twenties provided us with lots of opportunities to support each other in new ways, which ultimately strengthened our relationship.
Jodie: I agree with you... *when* you were stateside. You were very supportive when you could be, and if you hadn't been supportive...
Reggie: What? That wouldn't have worked for you?
Jodie: Um, no. That would have been no bueno. It would have caused me to doubt us. I mean, I was the one holding down the fort—paying the bills and taking care of the kids—while you were deployed for months on the other side

of the world. So if you weren't *fully* supporting me when you were home…

Reggie: All I was trying to say was this became a time of more mutual support opportunities, and even at a young age, we both understood that it was a give-and-take relationship.

Jodie: Erm…*ish*.

Reggie: What does "erm…*ish*" mean?

Jodie: Yes, we had opportunities to support each other in new ways and started to learn how to really give and take, but it was rocky at times. There was A LOT we didn't know, and we were trying to figure it all out without much external guidance. We were just feeling our way as best we could, and sometimes it was rather messy.

SEA AND SHORE TOURS

Every sailor in the Navy must go through an endless cycle of sea tours and shore tours. "Sea tours," as the name implies, means a sailor is stationed at sea more than they are at home. Sea tours are challenging and always live up to expectations. The lure of a shore tour *sounds* like a military member will be home more than away, but that isn't always the case, especially if a military member is in a competitive shore tour cycle. A shore tour cycle is often filled with unexpected times away from home. Often, a sailor will get into the rhythm of a shore tour, only to be ordered to go back to sea. The cycle begins anew every two to three years.

Sustaining a healthy relationship through both sea tours and shore tours is no joke. Jodie and Reggie spent so much time apart, including holidays, birthdays and anniversaries. While those special events are tough when separated, they discovered that missing each other in the everyday "mundane" things was often harder. Sleeping alone for months on end when the person you love is on the other side of the world becomes emotionally draining. The loneliness can overtake you if you let it. And although Reggie and Jodie had been in a long-distance relationship from the start, the stakes kept getting higher.

Reggie was in a competitive and dynamic workplace where only the top performers would have a future in the Navy. To ensure his family would have the best possible options at the conclusion of his tour, he needed to be ranked as the number-one performer. Competing for that top spot meant he had to perform in the office but also participate in non-work-hour activities. For Reggie, this meant a certain degree of going out and socializing, so everyone got to know who he was and what he was about. The social aspect of the workplace often became the deciding factor when all the work measurements were even.

From 1995 to 1998, Reggie was on a shore tour with no planned deployments. The expectation was that this would allow for more family time and a nine-to-five routine, but that wasn't always the case with increased social responsibility and Reggie's dynamic work ethic. It started to create a strain on their relationship. Jodie thought this would be a time for family, but the Navy was always calling, lingering in the background. The main challenge was establishing the right work-life balance.

The pressure of work-life balance continued to build. While their relationship felt mostly stable, there wasn't enough time for them to just be a couple. They hadn't even thought about taking time to enjoy each other outside of parenting and military functions. Date nights at home or having morning coffee together wasn't even on their radar. The busy work life and home life propelled their relationship along without a conscious awareness.

Moving through a relationship without intention creates challenges. They were so immersed in work, home, and family that they weren't prioritizing their relationship. They focused on the hustle and grind of daily life, and somewhere along the way, they were no longer on the same page or connecting meaningfully as a couple. It was often difficult to actually hear each other, even though they wanted to. It's as if they were speaking different languages.

> **Jodie:** Wouldn't it have been nice to know each other's love languages back then? Were love languages even a thing in the mid 90's?
> **Reggie:** What's your love language again?
> **Jodie:** [laughs] Very funny. But wouldn't it have been nice to know that we were *actually* speaking different languages to each other? And that we mostly spoke to each other in the language that we wished to be spoken to?
> **Reggie:** Yes, it would have been. Remind me, what's your love language again?
> **Jodie:** [laughing] You still don't remember? We've only been together for over thirty years.
> **Reggie:** Something service?
> **Jodie:** Acts of Service—meaning, rather than *telling* me you love me, *show* me. Show me the money, baby. That's how I feel loved.
> **Reggie:** Oh, that's right. That's why I do all the laundry in the house!
> **Jodie:** Exactly! I feel so loved and seen by you with every completed load.

Reggie: You must feel a LOT of love then!
Jodie: Oh, I do! I do!
Reggie: And what's mine again?
Jodie: [laughs] It makes me feel better that you don't know yours either.
Reggie: I'm nothing if not an equal opportunist.
Jodie: In our twenties, your love language was Words of Affirmation, followed closely by Physical Touch. Interestingly enough, yours has changed over the years, which can happen with love languages. Currently, you are also a big fan of Acts of Service—just like me—that's how you experience love.

A SECOND BLESSING

Reggie and Jodie always knew they wanted more children, but Jodie wanted to complete her degree before having another baby. Going to school with one child while Reggie was away was challenging enough, and the idea of bringing another baby into the mix seemed overwhelming.

Almost five years after the birth of Olivia, they had their second child, a beautiful baby boy named Grant, who was the best boy they could ever have. Grant fit right into the mix. He was a fabulous little man who showed up right on time, completing their beautiful family of four. At times, having a five-year age gap between their first and second child felt like they were starting over, but it also created lots of spaciousness to focus on both Olivia and the new baby.

As any couple knows, a new baby can shift the focus away from the relationship itself and place a strain on reconnecting with each other. While Jodie and Reggie didn't feel like there was anything "wrong" with their relationship, they weren't taking the time to nourish it either. When you aren't prioritizing your relationship, there can be a disconnection, and the cracks will start to show.

Jodie: Do you remember when I suggested that we go to couples counseling?
Reggie: I do, and I say, if it ain't broke, don't fix it.
Jodie: But if you don't maintain the relationship, it's *gonna* break. I was looking at counseling as maintenance, preventive health care, but you...
Reggie: It's a sign of weakness. We don't need no stranger telling us how to fix us
Jodie: It wasn't about getting fixed. It was about support. Neutral support. Interestingly enough, in a recent podcast episode, you surprised me and opened up about this. You shared that not only did you not want a stranger in our lives, but you also went on to say that you didn't want to be "wrong" or possibly called out by the therapist.
Reggie: [laughing] I don't recall any of that.
Jodie: Oh, it's in the podcast. You shared, half jokingly, and half not, that you believed the therapist would take sides, and you didn't want to be on the "losing" side.
Reggie: [laughing harder] Nope, none of that is ringing a bell.
Jodie: [laughing] Hmmmm... that doesn't sound like you? Wanting to be declared the winner of all things, all the time, especially with our arguments or disagreements?
Reggie: I can neither confirm nor deny.

Jodie: [laughs] Exactly. But here's the thing: people ask me all the time, "How do you get your spouse to participate in things like personal growth?" And the simple answer is—you don't. The secret is to focus on *yourself,* and your own personal growth. Not *theirs.* Focus only on what you can actually control. For me, that turned into my own personal development, mindset, and self-help work. Whether I read a book, took a class, went to a conference, or hired a professional. I started with me and my own healing journey and *that* has made all the difference.
Reggie: So I was right in not going to the therapist!
Jodie: Listen, I got where I needed to go, but I still believe it would have been a lot quicker and with a lot less frustration if you joined me from the beginning.
Reggie: But I got there.
Jodie: You did. And I am very grateful for that. But there weren't any guarantees that you would.
Reggie: C'mon, I wasn't gonna let you beat me. At some point, you knew I'd have to join you on the personal growth train.
Jodie: [laughs] I think you joined me because you realized that this train was going full steam ahead, with or without you.
Reggie: I'd never let you go without me.
Jodie: I'm really glad you didn't.

NAVY LIFE AMPS UP

Reggie continued to do well in every tour. As we were heading back out on a sea tour, he had been selected to be an admiral's aide. Some might call this a highly glorified personal assistant or secretary, but in the Navy, it's quite an honor to be an admiral's aide.

Reggie was very good at his job, but being an admiral's aide required a special skill set. I'd marvel at how he was always five steps ahead of what the admiral wanted. Reggie could always make it happen—whatever it was—with ease, or at least he always made it look that way. There were challenges with being an aide; mostly, it meant that he was gone more than ever. He was back on a sea tour, so we went back to letter writing. I would write him every night and drop the letters in the mail at the end of the week. It would take two weeks to reach him at sea, then another two weeks before I'd receive a return letter. A full month would pass before I'd get a response to my original concerns, questions, or news. By then, I had already forgotten what I'd written in my original letter. There was always something new to worry about, and he had no idea what I was dealing with because it would take weeks for him to learn about it. It gave me an interesting perspective, though. The things I had been so worried about or concerned with had shifted, worked themselves out, or changed completely by the time I received his response.

As hard as it was to have Reggie at sea for so long, the kids and I settled into a good groove. I had finished college and was able to focus on our little family. Olivia loved school and dance, and Grant was a curious and playful toddler. Looking back, I'm deeply aware that it was such a simple and blissful time.

Reggie: Life was so peaceful that you decided you wanted another baby.
Jodie: [laughs] Exactly! What better way to continue the peace than to have another baby?!
Reggie: But you wanted something extra with this baby.

Jodie: Listen, it wasn't so much as "extra" as it was a simple request.
Reggie: *Simple,* you say?
Jodie: Yes, it was the Navy's fault. I was just following their lead.
Reggie: Oh, is that how you saw it?
Jodie: Yes, I do. The Navy messed with me too many times. You know how I don't like being messed with, so I was simply trying to get ahead of them. Lucky for you, I needed your help to make it happen.

I was ushered into the unceremonious world of the government's healthcare system as soon as I became a military "dependent." Thankfully, each of my pregnancies had been uneventful, so I was a willing participant in the sterile obstetric experiences at each Navy hospital where we were stationed. I experienced impersonal and detached care. I never saw the same OB twice, and I never knew who I'd be seeing at each appointment. I didn't love this. I dreamed of having a midwife, or a water birth, or even the ability to get an epidural if I chose. The Navy only offered saddle blocks instead of epidurals, orderlies rather than nurses, and you were called by a number rather than your name. Still, I was young and healthy and, well... I didn't have a choice. Or so I thought.

The Navy had kicked me out of their healthcare system with my previous two pregnancies. Both times, they gave some sordid reason, like there wouldn't be enough room when it came time to deliver. Both times were during my third trimester. So with my two previous pregnancies, once in California and once in Florida, I was forced to scramble during my nesting phase to find new doctors to complete my OB care and deliver my babies.

Now it was 2000, I was pregnant with our third baby and I decided to take matters into my own hands. I wanted to experience civilian care from start to finish. I wasn't interested in getting kicked out by the Navy—again. So, I turned to Reggie to make it happen.

Jodie: I saw what an ah-mazing job you'd been doing getting the admiral everything and anything *he* wanted.
Reggie: Often before he even asked or knew he needed it.
Jodie: Exactly. You were so great at your job, so I wanted to give you the opportunity to do that for me, too. I asked you to arrange it so I could receive civilian care from day one with my third pregnancy—no military hospitals, no Navy doctors. Civilian care all the way.
Reggie: But it wasn't that simple. The Navy doesn't grant people civilian medical care just because they want it.
Jodie: Oh, I knew that, which is why I knew you were the person who could make it happen—if you wanted to.

ADMIRAL JODIE

When we were planning for the birth of our third child, Jodie had one request. She wanted to have this baby at a civilian hospital from the get-go. At this point, I was working as the admiral's personal assistant, but the job requirements were much more demanding than a typical assistant's duties. I handled all personal and professional tasks for him —his schedule, his wife's "honey-do" list—anything he needed. I always had to be five steps ahead and meet the admiral's needs. This made the job a little more intense than my previous position. "No" was never an acceptable answer. If he asked for it, he got it, and my challenge was to figure out how to get it for him.

Jodie watched me constantly pull rabbits out of hats and make the impossible possible for the admiral. Jodie wanted me to do the same for her, ensuring that our third child was born outside of the Navy system. After a month of inaction, Jodie and I had a very pointed conversation. She said to me, "You're a Navy person. You know how to get things done because there is a certain language and skill set to work within the system of the Navy. I need you to make this happen."

In a frustrated tone, I said, "The rules are the rules. What do you want me to do? I don't know what you expect me to do. We're going to have this baby in a Navy hospital, and there's nothing I can do to change that."

She looked me in the eye and said, "If the admiral was pregnant and told you he wanted to deliver at a civilian hospital, you'd make it happen without a second thought." At that point, I realized she was completely right. I would have found a way to make it happen for the admiral.

Within a couple of weeks of that eye-opening conversation, I found a way to make it happen for Jodie. It made me realize I was not in the right place and wasn't prioritizing my relationship with Jodie. That was a wake-up call. If she had made that request at the beginning of our relationship, I would have done anything to make it happen. How had I let myself get to a point where Jodie would ask me for something and I wouldn't do everything in my power to make it happen? I thought that was a very telling point in our evolution as a couple and in our relationship. I had somehow allowed myself to forget our number-one rule: us first, and everything else will work itself out.

Jodie: You know, it really was a good thing that you were able to get me the civilian care for the pregnancy.
Reggie: Oh, you don't have to tell me. I know it was.
Jodie: No, I mean, I know it was really good for our relationship, but it was also really good because of everything that went down with our third baby. Have you ever thought about that?
Reggie: Yeah, we had no idea what was on the horizon with baby number three.
Jodie: It's probably better that way.

FINAL THOUGHTS

This was an interesting and exciting phase of their life and relationship. They'd moved across the country. Reggie went from a shore tour to sea tour with a new baby thrown into the mix and Jodie's college graduation. During those times, Reggie and Jodie lost their way within the relationship, but they always managed to find their way back. The key to continuing to grow as a couple from the foundation they'd built was to always put their relationship first.

KEY TAKEAWAY

Focusing on your own personal growth is vital for a healthy relationship. Life will continually throw curve balls at you and your relationship, so being more in tune with yourself, understanding why you do the things you do and what makes you tick allows for greater ease, enjoyment, play, and understanding amidst the ups and downs that will inevitably come your way.

WHAT THEY WISH THEY HAD KNOWN: LOVE LANGUAGES

Do you ever feel like you and your partner can't *hear* each other? Like you are literally speaking different languages, or that you can't seem to get past *how* you speak to each other, so much so that nothing gets heard or worse, feelings get hurt? The truth is you are probably speaking different love languages.

Gary Chapman introduced the concept of The Five Love Languages with the idea being that people express and receive love in different ways. Understanding your own and your partner's love language will undoubtedly strengthen your relationship.

When Reggie and Jodie uncovered their love languages, their communication shifted and improved—dramatically. It created opportunities for them to be heard in new ways. Talking to each other in their unique love languages did take some getting used to, but with practice and patience, they both got the hang of it!

Jodie's love language is "Acts of Service." When Reggie became aware of this, he started to understand that seemingly mundane acts of service—doing the laundry, helping more with the kids, washing the dishes, feeding the dogs—made Jodie feel loved and seen in ways that saying the words "I love you" didn't.

Reggie's top love language, "Words of Affirmation," meant the exact opposite. When Jodie said things like "I'm proud of you" and "I appreciate you and all you do," it was deeply meaningful to

Reggie. When Jodie understood this, she began to use words of affirmation more freely.

One thing Reggie and Jodie have discovered is that your primary love language can change over time. For example, Reggie now identifies more with "Quality Time" than with "Words of Affirmation." So it is worthwhile to check back in with your love language and see if anything has shifted for you or your partner and to adjust accordingly..

> Learn more about Love Languages and how they have informed Jodie and Reggie's relationship by listening to: Episode 2: Love Languages of *Higher Love: The Podcast.*
> **SCAN THE QR CODE:**

SPECIAL BLESSINGS

Jodie: If you are pregnant, chances are someone will ask, "Are you having a boy or a girl?"

Reggie: Well, I always wanted a mini-me, so whenever anyone asked, I would say we were having a boy.

Jodie: What does that have to do with my question? But it's funny you say that because you did get two "mini-mes," and they are both girls.

Reggie: True.

Jodie: I think that was the universe's way of letting you know that what you want often shows up in unexpected forms, giving you exactly what you need. Can we get back to my initial question?

Reggie: What was it again?

Jodie: What's the typical response when people ask, "Are you having a boy or a girl?"

Reggie: "It doesn't matter, just as long as they're healthy."

Jodie: Correct. I remember when I used to say that, but

this leads to the *real* question: "What happens when you have a baby that's *not* healthy?"

Reggie: Now that's a tricky question...

Jodie: One that we unexpectedly found the answer to with our third baby.

Jodie had an uneventful routine pregnancy. For the first time, she received continuity of care from civilian medical providers from the very start. Everything had gone smoothly with the delivery. On December 20th, 2000, they received an early Christmas present—a beautiful baby girl, India Rose (Rosie), was born. She was the perfect addition to their growing family. Ten tiny fingers and toes, bright-eyed and alert, Reggie and Jodie couldn't help but beam at their newest blessing. The doctors and staff smiled as Rosie was declared perfectly healthy; even her newborn Apgar score was perfect. But then subtle signs began to hint at the trouble ahead.

It was our first night together, and Rosie and I were finally alone amidst the dull humming sounds of the hospital room. I marveled at her, taking in the sweet newborn smells, her jet-black hair, and her pink cheeks. But as I looked at her, something felt different. I couldn't put my finger on it exactly. But something felt off with Rosie compared to my other two babies. Maybe it was that she didn't have a strong grip when she held onto my finger, or how her head seemed much wobblier than I remembered with the others. I quieted this uncomfortable awareness by reminding myself that she had been declared fully healthy by the doctors, midwife, and nurses. Surely, I was just tired, and it had been a long day. Still, the nagging in my belly didn't want to go away.

As the next months and years of our lives began to unravel, I held onto this memory. It brought comfort and reminded me of the depth of a mother's intuition and how important it is to trust that above all else.

Over the next few months, Jodie's motherly intuition grew from a whisper to a scream. Something was indeed different. Something continued to feel off. Jodie couldn't put her finger on it, but she just "knew." Rosie was the sweetest, happiest baby, but she wasn't hitting any of her milestones. Every time Jodie took her for a wellness check, she shared her concerns with the pediatricians, but all they did was try to calm her nerves. They pointed out the things that were going well: Rosie was gaining weight, she was very engaging and happy, and she made great eye contact. They continually reassured her that Rosie was simply "taking her time."

Jodie was happy to hear this—she *needed* to hear this. Still, everything the doctors said went against her inner knowing. She really wanted to trust the doctors; after all, they were the experts.

No parent wants to hear that anything is "wrong" with their child. It is so much easier to believe that doctors and nurses know better, even when a deep inner voice and intuition have you thinking, *There's something wrong here.* Parents may not want to push back against medical professionals because the experts have seen hundreds, possibly thousands of babies, so surely they know better, right? The innate desire for their child to be healthy can take over and blind them until it can no longer be ignored.

One afternoon, while I was nursing Rosie, I noticed a twitching movement flow down the right side of her tiny body. As this unwelcome wave moved through her, she clenched her right hand into a tight fist. The wave then traveled down her right leg; she crunched up her belly and made an alarming guttural sound. I'd heard that same sound during her first month at home, but this time, I witnessed the wave. It was obvious she had no control over it, and it was terrifying. As I rushed her to the doctor, I had no idea how much our lives were about to change.

Jodie: We knew so little back then about how doctors and specialists and hospitals worked.
Reggie: It was probably just as well.
Jodie: True, I definitely didn't realize how concerned the pediatrician was when I rushed in that afternoon with Rosie and told her what I saw. She even got us an appointment with the neurologist the very next day. I mean, how could we have known?
Reggie: Well, we learned quickly. When you get an appointment with a neurologist or any pediatric specialist within twenty-four hours, it's no bueno. They are *mega* concerned.
Jodie: Yeah, the speed that we got that appointment was an extremely troubling indicator.
Reggie: As we would soon learn, those appointments can often take three to six months to get.
Jodie: And those months feel like an eternity when your child is going through something super troubling. The waiting lists are off the charts. But I guess ignorance is bliss because I would have been even more worried.

Reggie: And what would that "worrying" have done to help Rosie?

Jodie: Unfortunately, not a thing.

An EEG confirmed that there was seizure activity present. The neurologist immediately prescribed medication for six-month-old Rosie. Initially, Reggie and Jodie hesitated to give their infant the medicine. While they were both desperate to stop the seizure activity, they also wanted to understand more about the drug and any possible side effects.

Simply put, the doctors weren't very forthcoming with information. Their general attitude was that a doctor knows best, and if they were telling you to give your baby a prescribed medication, you should just do it. This was the year 2000 when WebMD and Google were in their infancy.

Jodie did her research as best she could. She went to the library, found medical journals, and read up on the drug. It was a helpless feeling to try to make informed decisions about her child's health, especially when time was of the essence. Ultimately, Jodie and Reggie decided to move forward with the medication. The good news: it controlled the complex partial seizures. The bad news: this heralded the beginning of Rosie's many health concerns.

Jodie: The doctors were so impatient with us for taking a few days to do some research and discuss the major decision of medicating our baby. They were rather annoyed that we wouldn't just blindly follow them.

Reggie: They didn't seem to understand that we aren't just blind followers.

Jodie: Taking that time was so important for us, both as parents and as a couple, and I'm so glad we did, despite the pressure coming from the "experts." We had no idea this would be the first of *many* instances over the upcoming years when we would need to take a stand.

Reggie: And not allow the medical system and its teams to run roughshod on us.

Jodie: Ultimately, it empowered us as a couple and as her parents. We quickly learned that we were her greatest, and sometimes her only, advocates. Many of the lessons we already learned about building our relationship really influenced how we were going to deal with Rosie's medical challenges in the years to come.

The following months became a landslide of unexpected health concerns. While the initial seizures were controlled with medication, a new and even more sinister type of seizure showed itself. Rosie was diagnosed with infantile spasms just a few months after the initial discovery and treatment of complex partial seizures. Sandwiched in between these two neurological disorders, Rosie was also diagnosed with a congenital heart defect, one that would eventually require cardiac surgery to repair. All the developmental delays that Jodie and Reggie had been witnessing since birth were finally being taken seriously by doctors and specialists.

I don't know if I ever felt so helpless in my life. I have two goals in life: be a wonderful husband and partner to my wife and be a supportive father for my kids. Math was my favorite subject growing up. I loved that if you correctly put information into a formula, you can get the right answer. Rosie's situation was a direct assault on that formula because there were many unknowns.

A fundamental piece in that puzzle was being a provider and someone my family could count on to help them solve their most perplexing problems. The initial period with Rosie really challenged that grading system. I could not solve this challenge for her. Hell, I was shooting her up with steroids. I guess I should explain that. One of the most challenging and heartbreaking periods in Rosie's medical journey was the decision to inject her daily with a steroid to relieve the infantile spasms. So we were juicing her with these growth hormones that the doctors told us would stop the seizures. The kicker was they couldn't tell us why it would stop them, just that it would. Every time I asked why it worked, their reply was, "We don't know; it just does." So we injected our nine-month-old baby girl every day for weeks, not knowing the long-term repercussions it could cause but knowing it was our only chance to tame the demon so we could get her healthy enough to have heart surgery.

The running joke was that I couldn't enroll her in any daddy-daughter sporting events because she would fail the urinalysis. I can laugh about it now, but there wasn't a lot of laughing going on then. I'm not sure if I have ever experienced a combination of frustration and failure like I did during that period.

Jodie: Yeah, there isn't a chapter about any of this in *What to Expect When You're Expecting*.

Reggie: The most frustrating part was that the doctors,

after missing so many of the signs that something was wrong, still had zero answers about how to fix things.

Jodie: Life kept spiraling and snowballing. It was like we would never get to the bottom of it. There were zero answers, despite all the specialists, hospital stays, and invasive tests. They couldn't tell us what had caused the seizures, the delays, the heart condition—none of it.

Reggie: It was crazy. It took years before they could even give us a diagnosis of cerebral palsy.

Jodie: During this time, our lives became unrecognizable. At the height of things, we were seeing eight different pediatric specialists, and if Rosie wasn't with a specialist, she was in PT, OT, or speech and language therapy. Every day was consumed with her medical needs and support. This time also fostered a ton of doubt in the medical community for us.

Reggie: But it also created a new level of trust within us. And, of course, none of this was happening in a vacuum.

IS THE FOUNDATION STRONG ENOUGH?

Reggie and Jodie attempted to keep their family focused and together, which was challenging with a child who had severe special needs. When the basic needs of one child are inherently greater than others, it could create adversity in the home. As parents, they needed to find a way to turn the newfound challenges into something that would help bring their family even closer.

They made a conscious effort to ensure that Rosie's needs didn't have a negative impact on the lives of her siblings, Olivia and Grant. Still, their kids grew up differently. They had an incredible amount of responsibility compared to other kids their age. They were continually asked to show up for their baby sister. They learned from a very early age to think of others before themselves and to have empathy for everyone.

Very early on, Reggie and Jodie started the conversation about the importance and necessity of coming together as a family on Rosie's behalf. Meeting her daily needs, from feeding her, dressing her, and keeping her safe, became a family affair. Rosie quickly became the lynchpin that brought them all together. They learned that "no" is a complete sentence. Many extra commitments started to fall by the wayside, and the only thing that truly mattered was their love for each other.

Jodie: I used to be concerned about the eight-year age gap between Olivia and Rosie and wondered how they were going to bond.
Reggie: Rosie took care of that.
Jodie: Yes, she did! She made sure the whole family was connected. The sheer power of who she is and how she moves through the world created a potency that none of us expected.
Reggie: She set the example for all of us from very early on.
Jodie: Even in the midst of all the trauma, I remember thinking that I wasn't going to be the one to rain on this baby's parade. Even when the specialists told me that she was never going to walk or achieve [XYZ], I wasn't going to feed into the story of everything that she *couldn't* do. I was

there to feed into everything she *could* do, and it was my job to help her do it.

Reggie: Yes. And to this day, she leads the way. She lives her life through love, connection, and joy.

Some doctors told me Rosie wouldn't walk. Others told me not to bother with potty training because she wouldn't be able to do it. Some doctors told me she'd never be able to speak or communicate. I would get so angry. She was still a baby, so how could they possibly think they knew everything that she would or wouldn't be able to do? They couldn't even come up with a proper diagnosis or tell me if the medication would work for her. But they wanted to predict her future? That's a hard no. This was long before I started any type of mindset work. Still, as her mother, I innately knew that I wasn't going to focus on all the limitations people were already placing on my child. Instead, I decided to focus on everything that she COULD do. I wasn't going to allow anyone to write her story for her. Just like everyone else, Rosie gets to write her own story.

As her mother, I will support, guide, and assist her as best I can, just like I do with my other children. Even though we were dealing with so much heartache, our family gets to write our own story. We all get to respond to and move through the unimaginable as we choose, not how it's prescribed by others. As we began to write our own story, we experienced beauty, compassion, and love through the unimaginable. With our help, Rosie is writing her story. She is living a truly original and exceptional life, one that we are lucky enough to be a part of.

Rosie's health challenges tested the foundation of their relationship more than anything so far. While Reggie and Jodie easily came together on Rosie's medical needs and how they incorporated her care with the rest of the family, they were each processing the circumstances on a deeper level.

When a parent has the realization that their child's life will be nothing like they envisioned, there is a deep grieving process that takes place. It takes time and patience to come to terms with the fact that a child will always be dependent for basic necessities, such as personal care, food, clothing, transportation, and total well-being. Reggie and Jodie were on very different timelines throughout this grieving process, each handling the internal and deeply emotional aspects of having a child with severe special needs in their own way.

———

Reggie: We grieve differently.
Jodie: Well, *I* actually work on processing the grief, but *you* prefer to push the grief down. So yes, you can say we grieve differently.
Reggie: [laughs] I'd always say, "It's going to be fine. Everything's going to be good." And you'd be like, "How do you know that?"
Jodie: Whenever you said that, I felt like you were bypassing your grief, that you didn't want to look at or deal with all the messy bits, and you preferred to jump to the "everything's gonna be alright" stage.
Reggie: But that's not true.
Jodie: Well, I know that *now*. But back then, I thought that if your grieving process didn't look like mine, then you must not be grieving. I wanted to see that you were

grieving because it was tearing me apart. I couldn't understand how it wasn't doing the same for you.

Reggie: Of course, it was doing the same to me.

Jodie: But you never wanted to share that with me or talk about it.

Reggie: Yeah, you want to feel all of it all the time.

Jodie: [laughs] I'm here to feel all the feels. Plus, I wanna talk about it... with you.

Reggie: I don't need to feel all that, and I really don't want to talk about it. I just need to know what the end is and let's just get there.

Jodie: This was when I wish I knew that your Gemini Moon was in the fourth house, which is a signifier of how deeply you *actually* feel things. Your astrological info would've been a game-changer. Plus, if I had also known I had a Libra Moon, I would've understood my deep desire for us to grieve *together*. Unfortunately, we didn't know any of this at the time, so we were just doing our best to hang on.

Reggie: But this did signify the real beginning of us trying to figure out many things. How do we communicate when something like this occurs? How do we honor each other's journey?

Jodie: It's definitely a vital journey as a couple. We fumbled a lot in those early years. My singular focus had to be on Rosie and the children. I'm sorry to say that I didn't have much bandwidth left for us or you.

Reggie: Oh, I know. "We" came second during those years. There weren't a lot of date nights or getaways.

Jodie: Unless you count hospital stays as weekend getaways.

Reggie: I do not.

Jodie: It's hard to make those places sexy.

Reggie: But I think the fact that we had such a solid foundation of love, trust, and togetherness helped us get through many of those things. It allowed us to make this experience the best it could possibly be for ourselves and our family.

Jodie: I agree, but it didn't come without some significant relationship casualties along the way.

FINAL THOUGHTS

Grief is different for everyone. There isn't a "right" way to move through the grieving process. It is, however, very important to acknowledge it, talk about it, and work through it instead of avoiding or bypassing it.

When a couple finds out that they are pregnant, visions of their child's future begin to fill their mind. But when those visions don't look like they expected, it can be both shocking and traumatic. It takes time, space, and grace to be able to let go of the hopes and dreams they've been carrying.

There isn't a "normal" out there, so creating a new one simply means you get to make it up as you go. You can figure out what works best for you and your family, readjusting and pivoting as needed. It helps to have a solid foundation as you pivot.

KEY TAKEAWAY

Trust yourself. Trust your partner. Trust your inner knowing. Trust that as a mother or father, you know what's best when it comes to your children. Experts are there to share their knowledge and offer guidance, but they do not get to override your intuition and your inner knowing.

WHAT THEY WISH THEY HAD KNOWN: A COURSE IN MIRACLES

When Reggie gifted Jodie a copy of *A Return to Love* by Marianne Williamson, he couldn't have known that he was opening the door to the singular text, *A Course in Miracles* (ACIM) by Dr. Helen Schucman, that would shift their lives more than anything else. *A Return to Love* is inspired by the teachings in ACIM, and when Jodie experienced such a deep transformation while reading *A Return to Love*, she decided to explore the text that inspired it.

ACIM is a non-denominational spiritual text. It offers a self-study program that focuses on the practice of forgiveness, the rejection of fear, and the acceptance of love as the ultimate truth. Jodie became an avid student of this spiritual text. It helped her navigate the ever-twisting and unpredictable path of raising a child with significant special needs. Some of the main concepts of ACIM are that "miracles are a shift in perception from fear to love" and "miracles occur naturally, every day." This understanding of a miracle, while at first foreign, eventually became a foundational belief for Jodie. When Jodie began to understand that we each have the ability to shift our own perspective—no matter what we are going through—she did her best to embody this truth, and with it, inner peace began to flow.

Jodie walked her own ACIM journey for many years before Reggie joined her, but when he did, their relationship shifted dramatically. Dr. Schucman's ACIM companion workbook for students became a part of their daily routine. Each morning, before they get out of bed, they listen to the daily lesson and take time for meditation together. The mindful act of beginning each day together brought them to a deeper, more soulful level of connection than ever before, and while ACIM doesn't guarantee their day will be perfect or that they won't disagree or be short with each other, it certainly ensures they are coming from the same grounded place of love and connection.

FORGING A NEW PATH... TOGETHER

After three tumultuous years of hospitalizations, countless specialists, and a multitude of therapy sessions, Jodie and Reggie were still no closer to a diagnosis for their daughter. So much time and energy had been put into uncovering what was "wrong," but nothing, in terms of an actual diagnosis, had actually been discovered. The only good news was that Rosie's medical needs started to settle a bit, and nothing new had presented in over a year. Between the oral medication and the growth hormone injections, the multiple seizure disorders were under control. Her cardiac surgery, although terribly stressful, had been a complete success. Her congenital heart defect was fully repaired. Rosie was gaining weight and growing, albeit slowly, but she was still making progress in those areas.

Life as they knew it had changed forever. It now took on an almost unrecognizable appearance. Medical equipment was strewn throughout the house, as walkers, wheelchairs, and pediatric braces all became a part of the regular landscape. Play was never just play; instead, it was a form of physical therapy or occupational therapy. There were long wait times in specialists' offices, sometimes five hours at a time. Rosie's medical case was no longer urgent; it was simply routine.

Reggie and Jodie stopped measuring milestones. Trying to compare Rosie's growth to a typical child was just too painful. It was hard to see how far behind she really was. Her cognitive development, in particular, seemed to be lagging behind more than her other milestones, and it seemed as if there was little they could do about it.

Somehow, in the midst of all the traumas and intensities, Reggie and Jodie uncovered a new normal. Being stationed in Jacksonville with family and friends close by created a vast support system. They could rely on this tremendous support system to be there at a moment's notice without a single hesitation, particularly when Reggie was gone due to his many duties with the Navy.

———

I was blessed to have such amazing friends, some from my military circle and others who weren't. Nonetheless, they all became family. I remember this one night when Rosie began throwing up blood. She was eleven months old and had recently finished her round of ACTH injections. The seizures had stopped, but she was still on a variety of other medications. She was prone to excessive spitting up, but she had never spit up blood. I needed to take her to the ER, but it was after midnight, and my other two children were sleeping. Reggie was away. I picked up the phone and called two friends, Kathy and Gloria. Kathy came over while Olivia and Grant slept, and Gloria met me and Rosie at the hospital. They both supported me without hesitation. They left their own families in the middle of the night to help me with mine. These are the types of friends I have, and I am forever grateful.

As powerful and strong as these types of friendships were, they started to come at a price. Little by little, I began to rely on my friends more than I would rely on Reggie. Yes, he was often gone during this time, but even when he was home, I shared more with my friends than with him. That had never been the case before. I used to always want to tell him everything first, especially if it had to do with the kids. But when he'd call from the other side of the world to hear about a specialist appointment, I had little desire to relive it with him and barely talked about it. Instead of calling him first about Rosie's test results, I'd call my friends. I knew I could count on them. I knew they'd be there, even to help me in the middle of the night, but the sad truth was that I wasn't sure Reggie could be around.

At first, Rosie's challenges brought us together, but then I was left behind to deal with all the appointments, specialists, therapists, and insurance issues. The stress started to wear down our relationship. We were both hurting so much, and sometimes it was easier to "not" be together. Sometimes, it was easier to deal with the pain and sadness when we were apart or when I was with a friend because when we were together, our sadness was often amplified. We had lost our way in terms of how to be there for each other. And even though we both knew this and wanted to change things because it was tearing us up inside, we couldn't seem to find our way back to each other.

THE NAVY KEEPS CALLING

Because I had done well in all my Navy jobs, I was on the path to achieving my goal of becoming a squadron commanding officer. To give myself the best chance of success, my boss advised me to take orders to the Pentagon in Washington, D.C. He presented me with three options:

- **Option A:** Take orders to the Pentagon, which would give me the best chance to continue to advance to squadron commanding officer.
- **Option B:** Take orders to the command post in Jacksonville to be the Chief of Staff for the Wing commander. These orders would still give me a pretty good chance to advance, but the odds of advancing would be lower than with Option A.
- **Option C:** Take orders to a Wing staff position at the command post in Jacksonville. This position would be less demanding than the Chief of Staff position. My quality of life would be really good, but I was pretty much telling the decision-makers that I didn't want to compete for squadron command anymore.

Options B and C kept us in Jacksonville, and Option A would take us to D.C. Jodie and I had been discussing the pros and cons of the decision for about a week.

Finally, I said, "Honey, I have to give the boss an answer by COB Friday. Do you want to move to D.C., or do you want to stay in Jax?"

Jodie did not want to leave Jacksonville. She believed it was best for Rosie and the rest of the family to keep our environment consistent while we continued to navigate Rosie's medical journey. So I told my boss our decision.

He said, "Are you sure, Reggie? Because Option A opportunities don't come along very often." I told him I still had a shot at command with the Option B orders, and it was better for my family if we stayed in Jacksonville. To his credit, he understood and was very supportive of the decision.

Reggie: This all went down at work on a Friday afternoon.
Jodie: You came home to tell me that you talked to your boss, and since it was what you and I had already decided, you were very much at peace with it.
Reggie: I was.
Jodie: Initially, I was too. But then, over the course of the weekend, something in me shifted.
Reggie: I just wish it had shifted *before* I went into my boss's office and turned down the Pentagon orders.
Jodie: [laughing] That would have made things easier, but what kind of story would it be then? Plus, I've come to learn that once an immediate need gets met, you sometimes realize that maybe it wasn't the thing you actually needed after all.
Reggie: [laughing] Or maybe you just wanted to see what you could make your husband do and prove your power over me every now and again?

That weekend, something became crystal clear to me: if we stayed in Jacksonville for another tour and kept going the way we were, our marriage would suffer greatly, and it might not make it. I remember this being a significant turning point for me in our relationship because I understood that I needed to somehow create space to rely on Reggie again. I had become so independent. I often felt like I didn't even need him. I was in pure survival mode. I had gotten so used to handling all the things, all by myself, that even when he was home, I wouldn't include him. It was exhausting but it had become my everyday reality. Part of me wanted to let him back in but wasn't sure how or if I even could. Somewhere deep inside of me, though, I knew that I wanted my partner back. I was willing to take a chance on us and knew that started with me being more vulnerable and more honest with him.

———

Reggie: So instead of allowing our relationship to slowly drift into the great void of destruction, you made me go back to my boss, who I had just told three days earlier that there was no way in the world we were ever going to change our mind.

Jodie: [sheepishly] But I did change *our* mind. And then, late that Sunday evening, I broke it to you that I actually wanted to go to D.C.

Reggie: I was like, "You've got to be shitting me..."

Jodie: [laughs] I know, it was rough. I wasn't even able to verbalize all the reasoning behind it at first.

Reggie: Uh, yeah... you just said, "We need to take those orders."

Jodie: I was still processing everything at that time, but that weekend, something in me shifted, and I had to honor it. I had no idea how it would all turn out, or if it would even work out, but I just knew that we needed to go. I knew that you and I needed to have a new adventure —*together*.

Reggie: We do have a pattern of doing really well when it's just us figuring stuff out.

Jodie: I wasn't totally sure how, but all I remember thinking was that a move will bring us back together.

Reggie: So we moved.

Jodie: We moved away from all of Rosie's doctors and

specialists, her therapies, and all the friends and family that supported us.

Reggie: You were ready to leave it all.

Jodie: I was terrified, but I was ready to turn everything upside down and start fresh and hopefully find "us" in the process.

Reggie: On Monday morning, I went back to my boss and told him that we'd changed our mind.

Jodie: I bet that was an uncomfortable conversation.

Reggie: He laughed and said, "Yeah, I didn't turn those orders off yet. I was going to wait through the weekend. I was going to make a call tomorrow if you didn't come back."

Jodie: You see? The universe had our backs, and it all worked out.

BE CAREFUL WHAT YOU ASK FOR

In the summer of 2003, Reggie and Jodie left everything they knew behind. They left Jacksonville and made their way to Northern Virginia, where Reggie was officially stationed at the Pentagon in Washington, D.C. It was their first time living in a non-Navy environment. Reggie quickly realized that working in the Pentagon was nothing like working in the fleet Navy. There weren't any squadron mates or social activities. The Pentagon was all business.

Jodie and the kids enjoyed a complete break from the Navy lifestyle. Living in the suburbs of Northern Virginia, no one cared about what Reggie did or that he was in the Navy. Jodie worked to find new doctors in D.C. for Rosie. She hoped they would be able to shed new light on Rosie's medical concerns and finally come up with a diagnosis. Although D.C. was a major medical hub, they were disappointed when the specialists didn't have much more to offer. The wait times for an appointment were even longer than they were in Jacksonville. The D.C. doctors ran the same blood tests, muscle biopsies, and scans all again with very little new findings.

Frustration ran high. Reggie and Jodie wanted to find some solutions, yet the doctors had few answers. They decided to make trips further up the east coast to Kennedy Krieger Institute in Maryland and Nemours Children's Clinic in Delaware in search of new doctors in the hope of finding actual answers. These trips proved to be just as fruitless.

In the fall of 2005, even though there were no new symptoms, Rosie's D.C. neurologist suggested ordering *another* MRI of her brain. Multiple MRIs had been performed since Rosie was a baby. She had to undergo sedation and endure a lengthy hospital visit each time. Reggie and Jodie debated whether putting Rosie through yet another invasive procedure would be worth it, but they decided to say yes. And it was with this MRI, when she was almost 6 years old, that a radiologist was able to determine she had suffered from a "one-time insult or injury that led to a lack of oxygen in the developing brain." The actual "insult or injury" was never determined.

The neurologist explained that this evidence had been present all along, that it had most likely occurred before birth, and each MRI would have shown it, but that all the other radiologists had simply "missed" it when reading her previous MRI results. The neurologist casually went on to explain that if this had been discovered earlier, Rosie wouldn't have undergone quite as many invasive procedures and that this type of finding allowed him to safely declare the diagnosis of—Cerebral Palsy (CP).

Cerebral Palsy is a group of neurological disorders that permanently affect a person's ability to move, balance, and maintain posture. Approximately 40–50 percent of individuals with CP have an intellectual disability. CP is not progressive—however, there is no cure for it.

Jodie: I had a huge misconception about the medical field. I thought someone—maybe one of Rosie's *seven* specialists—was attempting to put all the pieces of this medical mystery together.
Reggie: They certainly weren't doing it in the seven minutes we would actually see them. They barely remembered her name and would actually read her chart right there in front of us to "refresh" their memory of where they had left off.
Jodie: I will never understand why they couldn't take five minutes to review the chart *before* they walked into the exam room.
Reggie: They'd already kept us waiting for hours, so another five minutes wouldn't have made a difference.
Jodie: Right, and they would have at least *looked* like they were prepared to see us.
Reggie: Or that they actually remembered our kid and her medical case.
Jodie: That would have been comforting.
Reggie: Screw comfort. It would have made them look competent.
Jodie: That too. But the truth was, no one was trying to weave everything together. So I decided to do it myself.
Reggie: You were your own Dr. House.

Jodie: Oh! I loved that show! Before we finally got a diagnosis, I became my own sort of medical expert. I had a huge binder filled with copies of the clinic notes and lab results that I had requested. I'd comb through it regularly, trying to make sense of it all.

Reggie: Then you'd bring that big-ass binder to every doctor appointment.

Jodie: I did, and they loved it! How many times did those specialists *thank* me for my binder and use *my* highlighted notes to navigate Rosie's appointment?

Reggie: Too many.

Jodie: Keeping all her medical records in order and attempting to solve this puzzle became a full-time job. As a mom, I felt my job was to help my child as best I could. The problem was I was coming at it from the wrong angle. I thought helping her meant that I needed to *fix* things. It took me a while, but I finally realized that Rosie wasn't broken. She didn't need me, or anyone, to *fix* her.

I believe that a miracle is a shift in thinking from fear to love. For me, that shift—that miracle—occurred when I realized that my child wasn't broken. Instead of devoting energy to solving something that wasn't broken, I was able to experience her in a totally new way. I started to understand that my job was to support her and create the most loving environment, but I didn't need to fix her. Slowly, the pressure of all the things that she wasn't doing—walking, potty training, talking— started to melt away. I stopped trying to make her into something she wasn't, and I was finally able to see her for who she was. I allowed her to simply be, knowing that her life would not look anything like the rest of our lives, but that's okay. It's even more than okay—it's spectacular. The life she leads and the blessings she bestows are truly out of this world.

ALL WORK, NO PLAY

Unlike my previous jobs, the Pentagon was all business, and there wasn't much after-work socializing. I really struggled during this time. Work started at 6:00 a.m. and usually ended between 7:00 and 8:00 p.m. I am a social person, and I was determined to get some outside fun going, so I designated a local Irish bar as the unofficial officers club of the Pentagon. I created events to motivate people to come out.

At the time, I thought I was creating this environment for everyone else, but I later realized I was really doing it for me. I had come to depend on work and after-work activities as a way to escape the difficult issues I was facing at home. It had become my way of dealing with the frustration, powerless feelings, and feelings of inadequacy regarding Rosie's medical situation. Next thing you know, I was working long hours, hosting social gatherings, and running on about five hours of sleep.

Everything finally came to a head when I got into a pretty serious car accident because I was fatigued. I wasn't injured, but only by the grace of God. The accident led me to do some real soul-searching about how I could allow such an event to happen, bringing more stress to a home already burdened with multiple stressors. I realized a lot of this was me trying to escape. As a father and a parent, my responsibility is to help my kids and to make sure they have a better life than the one I had. My job is to help them be the best version of themselves. I didn't know how to do that with Rosie. I felt like I wasn't being a good dad because I couldn't figure that out for her. After the accident, I recognized that the best way to deal with these complex emotions and feelings was to lean on and rely even more on my relationship with Jodie. I believe the accident happened to wake me up and open my eyes to certain lessons. I was glad that I was receptive to learning those lessons so they wouldn't grow into even bigger issues.

Moving brought Jodie and Reggie back together. They faced many new challenges and took them on together as a couple. They chose to join forces again. Reggie was around more often. Jodie found herself actively relying on him. Whether it was attending a doctor's appointment or exploring Northern Virginia, they were experiencing more of life together.

Reggie: Leaving Jacksonville helped us get back on the same page.
Jodie: You're welcome! Ha! But seriously, not having our friends and family forced us to reconnect and remember just how good of a team we really are. We were able to access the public school system and had a lovely house in a great neighborhood.
Reggie: You mean "Pleasantville."
Jodie: Yes, I loved raising our kids in Pleasantville. I fell in love with Northern Virginia, and I was starting to live my best life. I did feel bad about your long work hours and the commute, though.
Reggie: [laughing] You mean me having to wake up at 4:30 to be at the Pentagon for my 6:00 a.m. brief and not getting home till dark?
Jodie: Yeah, that kinda sucked. But we had nights and

weekends, and you didn't deploy, and you could actually take leave when you wanted. There were some decent bonuses to the Pentagon. Plus, as always, work was going really well.
Reggie: True, I picked up Command during this time.

Reggie got selected to become the commanding officer (CO) of a squadron. It was a tough selection process and the job he had been working toward for years. It was a huge accomplishment and truly an honor to be selected. As a commanding officer, Reggie was in charge of a fleet of planes and hundreds of people. He made real changes and affected lives in a positive way. Becoming a commanding officer was the highest achievement he could attain at that point in his military career.

Reggie: We were excited.
Jodie: Erm, some of us were more excited than the rest of us. [laughs] Actually, I was very excited for you. This was something you had worked toward.
Reggie: Something *we* had worked toward.
Jodie: Right. And it was an amazing position. We'd seen firsthand the real difference that a commanding officer can make in the lives of so many.
Reggie: We saw that difference could be really good, and that became our goal. We wanted to make the experience with the squadron comparable to what we had on our first squadron tour.

Jodie: Yes, we knew right away that was going to be our priority.

Reggie: And because of the way the Navy is set up and the fierceness of the competition, the COs can get off track sometimes. They're in command of missions, planes, and people, but they lose track. The people are always the priority, and I knew I was going to prioritize my people... always.

Jodie: And you did.

Reggie: But the truth was, the prospect of being a CO was always a little more enjoyable for me than for you.

Jodie: [laughing] Ya think?

Reggie: Yeah, any position where you'll be referred to as a "COW" (Commanding Officer's Wife) is not the most inviting.

Jodie: That's not really my idea of a good time. I enjoy being a part of the team, especially when it's your team. I knew it would be a worthwhile endeavor and that, together, we could make a difference in the lives of sailors, officers, and their families—just as our favorite commanding officers and their spouses did in ours. That, at least, gave me something to focus on.

Becoming the commanding officer of an operational squadron also meant that Reggie and Jodie would have to leave Northern Virginia. For Reggie, this was the biggest promotion of his life. For Jodie, it meant leaving her cocooned "Pleasantville," where no one cared about who she was or what her husband did. It meant leaving the house she loved and taking the children out of the community where they were thriving. It also meant she'd now be known as a "COW" (Commanding Officer's Wife).

The Navy assigned Reggie to be the CO of a squadron in Jacksonville, Florida. Heading back to a military base and city they were familiar with was helpful, but it also created challenges. They were returning to the same place they had left just a few years ago. Jodie was now concerned that many of the old pressures would return, and she and Reggie would fall back into their old ways and disconnect from each other.

FINAL THOUGHTS

During this period, Jodie and Reggie learned from their great teacher, Rosie, that normal is different for everyone and happiness is not defined solely in fairytales or traditional ways. Rosie's ever-present joy taught them to really appreciate the simple things in life and to ENJOY them. Rosie was, and is, labeled as *disabled*, but that is the very last word that applies to her. She taught their entire family how to enjoy life and celebrate every tiny detail for the miracle that it is. She showed what it truly means to love unconditionally, which helped Jodie and Reggie appreciate and value their relationship. They did not take each other for granted, and they valued the little things they did for each other, like making up the bed or putting away the dishes. The small things allow for the enjoyment of all things.

KEY TAKEAWAY

Getting vulnerable and being honest with each other—no matter how messy or uncomfortable it is—is always a good idea.

WHAT THEY WISH THEY HAD KNOWN: WABI-SABI LOVE

Wabi-sabi is the ancient aesthetic philosophy of finding beauty in imperfection. Wabi-sabi is the practice of embracing that which is natural, raw, and unfiltered. It is the pursuit of uncovering beauty in things that have been marred by time. Reggie and Jodie have discovered that the ancient wisdom of wabi-sabi can be just as useful for relationships as it is for appreciating art.

Discovering the art of wabi-sabi invited Reggie and Jodie to embrace the concept of impermanence. It reminded them their relationship was fluid and ever-evolving. Wabi-sabi also reminded them that it was up to *them* to be willing to adapt and make changes as their relationship required. It ultimately brought their focus and awareness to all the opportunities for growth and renewal, rather than stagnation, that live within their relationship on a daily basis.

Wabi-sabi encouraged them to place value on the seemingly mundane aspects of the everyday. Little things like sitting together for morning coffee are elevated to a whole new level of connection and enjoyment when viewed through the lens of wabi-sabi.

For Jodie and Reggie, practicing wabi-sabi love also allowed them to bring an air of lightheartedness to some of their "annoying" quirks. It used to drive Jodie crazy that Reggie preferred to pick up, organize, and fold the *dirty* clothes on the bathroom floor rather than toss them into the dirty clothes basket, which caused much confusion when it came time to do the laundry.

In turn, it drove Reggie crazy that Jodie would never leave the car keys on the back of the kitchen door. He always had to search for them—first by locating her purse somewhere in the house, then digging through her bag to find the keys whenever he needed to move the car, usually early in the morning or late at night.

When they began to shift their focus and chose to highlight the humor in these eccentricities, the frustration and annoyance began to melt away—or at least lessen. When they started to see little imperfections as added value rather than a detriment, they began to appreciate the private beauty of their relationship and anchor into a deeper level of authenticity, love, and life.

Learn more about wabi-sabi love and how it has informed Jodie and Reggie's relationship by listening to: Episode 4: Wabi-sabi Love of *Higher Love: The Podcast.*
SCAN THE QR CODE:

NO FOX LIKE A MAD FOX

Jodie: You whisked me and the kids away from our happy cocoon, our insulated life in suburbia, when you were promoted to commanding officer. We basically went from a family of five to a family of—

Reggie: About five thousand.

Jodie: You were in charge of lots of people, lots of planes, LOTS of big decisions.

Reggie: And you were being celebrated as a COW.

Jodie: Cringe, just cringe. How antiquated is that?! The Commanding Officer's Wife had the illustrious title of being called a "COW."

Reggie: Yeah, you were never a fan of that title.

Jodie: Would you be?

Reggie: [laughs] I can't say that I would.

Jodie: The good part was that we were moving back to Jacksonville. I knew the lay of the land, still had friends in the area, and we were closer to family again.

Reggie: Right, and we were going to live on the Navy base.

Jodie: [Hmph] One step further into my fishbowl existence for the next few years.

Reggie: Well, at least we had a good idea where Olivia and Grant would go to school.

Jodie: Still, the biggest question and greatest concern was where Rosie would go to school.

As a military mom, my top priority when stationed somewhere new was to find the best schools for my kids. Living in Northern Virginia, just outside of D.C., we were blessed to have an excellent public education system. Rosie was placed in Early Childhood programs and loved going to school. Our goal for her was always full inclusion, where she would be able to learn alongside her typically developing peers. We experienced this with the public school system in Northern Virginia. In Florida, not so much. I would have gladly paid for her to attend a private school, but the level of care she required was too much for the private schools.

While in Command, Reggie and I had many meetings with classroom teachers, principals, and the head of the school board in an effort to meet Rosie's educational needs. For the most part, they were ill-equipped. They still believed that "separate is equal" when it came to special needs education and couldn't wrap their heads around the fact that my then kindergartener with special needs had every right to sit in a general education classroom alongside typically developing peers. In Florida, demanding her rights was often a fight, one that Reggie and I willingly took on together.

In addition to taking on the Special Education Department of Duval County Public Schools, Reggie and Jodie's other children, Olivia and Grant, were once again dealing with the upheaval of being the "new" kids at school. Providing support and assisting their children's transition was of utmost importance. At the core of their parenting, they always came together to ensure that all their children's needs were met in the best way possible. When they disagreed on parenting styles, they would talk to each other first, in private, to understand each other's parenting decisions before saying anything to their children.

It wasn't always easy, especially when there were so many responsibilities outside of the home. They had to be united on the parenting front so each child received a consistent message. Their goal was to keep the lines of communication with their children as open as possible. No topic was off the table. They wanted their children to feel comfortable about sharing what was bothering them or what was going on in their lives. They also tried to make their expectations and roles in the family unit clear.

Their kids grew up differently than many of their peers. They took on a lot of extra responsibility because they had a sister with severe special needs. Whenever they attended family parties or a Navy function, Jodie and Reggie would bring all the kids. Rosie loved being social. Even at a party, Grant and Olivia looked out for their baby sister to make sure she was being included and participating with the other children. This type of responsibility amped up when Reggie became the commanding officer. There were a lot more events, sometimes hosting hundreds of people and often in their home. Along with all the work Jodie put into creating and hosting, Olivia and Grant had additional responsibilities to entertain other people's children. They didn't always love doing this. Still, it was about everyone doing their part in the family unit and coming together.

Jodie: When people meet our family now, they often ask, "How did you raise such empathetic and caring adults who really like each other?"

Reggie: Well, I think all of these things forced Olivia and Grant to be a little more mature. Especially as teens and tweens, when you feel like the whole world is meant to revolve around you, they had to actually live outside of themselves.

Jodie: They saw early on that just because someone does something differently than you—whether it's how they walk or talk or move through the world—it doesn't make them *less* than you. Our children live and breathe with this understanding.

Reggie: I also think how we raised them and always included them in our lives was important.

Jodie: Right. Creating a family that loves, respects, and actively enjoys each other doesn't just happen. It has to be a strong combo of nature and nurture.

As stressful and time-consuming as running a squadron was, Reggie was quite good at it. As with most challenges, Reggie and Jodie came together for the betterment of those involved and prioritized the things most in need of their attention. They created a robust and successful squadron life and did their best to ensure that everyone felt included. For Jodie, this endeavor was a labor of love, and she cherished those times when she could just be "Jodie" and not the "COW." There were some days in particular that allowed her to feel blissfully ordinary.

CHOOSING EACH OTHER EVERY DAY

In the autumn of 2007, Reggie was deployed to Japan as the commanding officer. It was our second school year back in Jacksonville. We should have been more settled, but after the terrible experiences with Rosie's previous elementary school, I had spent the summer scrambling to find a new school for her. Thankfully, I found a small charter school that was willing and mostly capable of having Rosie as a student. Grant could also attend the same school, which was promising.

I was tentative about another new school. I was still dealing with the trauma from the previous school year but was hopeful that things could be better. Honestly, they couldn't get worse. I was also very relieved. The charter school wasn't too far from the Navy base, and I wouldn't have to drive all three kids to and from three different locations for the entire school year. Rosie's kindergarten teacher, while welcoming and kind, had never had a student like her. I spent many hours in conferences at the start of the year, expressing her needs and ensuring they were being met.

Grant was doing a pretty good job adjusting to his second new school in as many years. As a resilient and easy-going fourth grader, he was making new friends. He often talked about a girl who seemed to really like him. She kept asking him if she could come over to the house for a playdate, but he had no interest in playing with her.

A few months had passed, and we were all still finding our footing at the new school. Evenings and weekends felt very long when Reggie was gone. One weekend, there was a school-sponsored event. Since the start of the school year, my focus had been helping Rosie adjust, so I was looking forward to meeting some of Grant's new friends and their parents because I wanted to start establishing relationships with them. During the event, I took Rosie to the restroom. There wasn't a large handicapped stall, so we squeezed into a small but clean one. At this time, Rosie still needed full support holding herself up to use the restroom. As I squatted in the stall to hold her, I glanced to my left. There, scribbled in black, bold Sharpie, were the words: "I LOVE GRANT MICHAEL HOWARD." *I just about dropped Rosie and fell on the floor! I couldn't believe it.*

I stared at the graffiti while I patiently waited for Rosie to use the restroom. Then it really hit me. Even though I was dealing with tons of medical and school stuff for Rosie, and Reggie was stationed on the other side of the world, our easy-going, never-complaining nine-year-old boy was also dealing with real-life stuff, and I needed to make sure I was carving out time to be there for him too. I needed to ensure I was asking him more about the deeper workings of his life and the many stressors that he was also dealing with.

NO FOX LIKE A MAD FOX

Reggie had hit a huge milestone in his career when he was promoted to commanding officer, which he had been working towards for over a decade. However, with this promotion, his work-life balance was going to be mostly non-existent for the next few years. It meant that Reggie's and Jodie's attention and physical presence were going to be in higher demand outside the home. Their goal was to create a squadron life that felt like a family, one that felt like a true community.

When a military person is part of a squadron and on a sea tour, they can expect long separations from family and home. It is a stressful time, not only for the military members, but also for their family. When a squadron is deployed, they are often at the tip of the spear, meaning they are in hostile and unstable locations throughout the world. As the commanding officer, Reggie was responsible for leading his team in the successful execution of all missions they were assigned. Many of these missions placed his team members in harm's way with the possibility that they may not survive. Reggie and Jodie understood the necessity and power of creating a family-like environment within the squadron itself. For Jodie especially, this included helping the spouses and children feel stabilized and grounded during this stressful time.

> **Jodie:** The squadron and its many needs became a HUGE part of our decision-making process.
> **Reggie:** Creating a family environment with thousands of people takes a lot of energy and effort.
> **Jodie:** It doesn't just happen.
> **Reggie** And, honestly, that vision is not the norm.
> **Jodie:** But that was what we experienced in the early nineties with our first squadron when we were first married and just starting out. Honestly, it made all the difference.
> **Reggie:** It really did. Even though it wasn't the norm, we knew it was what we wanted to do.
> **Jodie:** We often seem to find ourselves on the path less traveled.
> **Reggie:** Because it requires the most. Being in command of a squadron was more than a job; it was a calling of sorts.
> **Jodie:** We put in a ton of effort to make your squadron and its family life the best that it could be. It became a full-time job for me—one that I was happy to do but oh so glad to be rid of in a few years!
> **Reggie:** I could have stayed in that job forever.
> **Jodie:** I know. You loved every minute of it. For me, it

became untenable after a while, and in many ways, it was pulling us apart as a couple.

Reggie: That was kind of your fear going into the whole thing.

Jodie: Rightfully so! Your role required you to focus on a lot of other people and places—other than me and us. I, too, was focused on many things. Neither of us was in a place to prioritize the needs of our relationship or make time for just you and me as a couple.

Reggie: [laughs] What'd ya mean? You didn't appreciate getting dressed up and going to all of those military galas and events with me?!

Jodie: [Ha-ha] I mean, it was mostly fun and sometimes glamorous, but it wasn't very romantic. It wasn't personal; it was work. I always had to be "on," and it certainly didn't leave a whole lot of time for just the two of us.

Finding time for the squadron and my family in the required allotments was extremely challenging during this period. I had a clear idea of how I wanted my time in the squadron to be set up. Throughout my naval career, I had been observing and developing tools and techniques to create a great squadron environment. To effectively lead a group of people, they must believe that you actually care about them. The best way to show I cared was by spending time with the squadron members and learning about their hopes and dreams. To reach my own goals, I needed to invest time in the squadron, which meant that my family ended up getting less of my time.

One morning, Jodie asked if we could have a date night. I responded, "I can't tonight because I'll be in the squadron from midnight till five in the morning." Jodie furrowed her brow and wanted to know why I was doing that. I said, "Because that's what the sailors who work the night shift need to see from me. Every member, whether they work during the day when everyone is around or at night when no one is around, is a key to the squadron's success. It is challenging for the night shift team to believe I care when they never see me except when it's convenient for me." While doing something that I wasn't required to do was a major inconvenience for me and my family, my actions showed the squadron that I cared.

Reggie and Jodie had a clear vision of the type of squadron life they wanted to create before starting command. And, for the most part, they were able to execute it. What they had failed to realize was how the demands of the command—along with raising a family, navigating a variety of special needs concerns, and Reggie being deployed—would affect them as a couple.

Coming together for the squadron? Easy. Coming together for their children? Easier. Coming together just for them? Somehow, it wasn't easy at all. They needed to figure out how their relationship fit into all of this.

Jodie: We could not have understood that even though we were in lockstep with everything else, it was going to tear away at our personal connection.
Reggie: Well, we'd never done anything like this before, so there wasn't really any way for us to see the kind of wear and tear it could possibly bring.
Jodie: Yeah, It's probably better that way, or I would have been an even less willing participant.

Reggie: We had never prioritized anything above us that wasn't related to our children before now.

Jodie: That second year in command was really tough for me. I started to feel disconnected from you, and worse, I wasn't sure how to get it back. It was odd because we were in lockstep with the squadron and even family goals, but somewhere along the way, we lost a little bit of us.

In a sea of over five hundred people, I started to feel very alone. Once again, I was relying less and less on Reggie. Although I was giving the squadron and our family my all, I was losing myself in the process. I still had friends in Jacksonville, but due to the nature of squadron life, the stress with Rosie's school, and our family's needs, I didn't have a ton of time or energy to hang out with my network of people. Some of my friendships began to fall away, and even though I knew it was happening, I didn't have the bandwidth to stop it. At times, I felt like I was barely holding it all together. I started losing weight and wasn't eating well. I wasn't taking care of myself. The much-needed aspects of self-care hadn't entered my awareness. Often, I was running on fumes. I tried to keep my eye on the ball and my mind on the mission, but the ongoing duties and requirements of our military life were exhausting. I'd pulled away from my support network to the point where I had very few people I could count on. It was a lonely time—one that I am glad lasted for only two years. The fact that I knew it would come to an end was the motivator to get me through. I kept a countdown in my head and when I was feeling particularly lonely or down, I would remind myself that this was all temporary.

THE END OF AN ERA

Reggie: I felt accomplished at the end of that command tour. We had given it our all and succeeded in doing the things we said we would do. We did it! By this point, I started getting that vibe from you that was like, "I'm good."
Jodie: You mean the "I'm *done* with this Navy stuff" vibe? Because *that* was definitely the vibe I was giving [laughs].
Reggie: [laughs] Yeah, but I was thinking, *I have so much more to give. This went really, really well, and there are more ways to help.*
Jodie: You always want to help.
Reggie: I do!
Jodie: It's one of your gifts, and I really love you for it. I just felt like I had little more that I could actually give to this navy life.
Reggie: Yeah, I knew I had to get you out of Jacksonville and back to your happy place in Northern Virginia, so I took another set of orders to the Pentagon in D.C.
Jodie: Where nobody knows my name or cares what your military rank was or that you're even in the Navy.
Reggie: [sighs] Yes, and I got to drive an hour each way to work with the "man" in the Pentagon every day.
Jodie: All I know is, when we were done with squadron life, I felt like a totally new person. It was a breath of fresh air to be back in my house with the kids back at really good schools. My life became my own again. I had the bandwidth to think about what I wanted. And I totally surprised myself by realizing that what I really wanted—another baby.

FINAL THOUGHTS

This period of their lives was characterized by service and sacrifice. From being in command of a squadron to raising young children and a teenager, it was easy to get lost in meeting the needs of others. Jodie and Reggie tried to create memories and experiences for their family and their work family. Once again, with so many competing priorities, they put their relationship at the bottom of the priority list. What helped them get through it was knowing that this was only temporary.

KEY TAKEAWAY

Open lines of communication with children are key and must be faithfully maintained and nurtured. Creating a family that loves, respects, and actively enjoys each other doesn't just happen. It requires vigilance, intention, and unwavering commitment.

WHAT THEY WISH THEY HAD KNOWN: "3 THINGS PLUS 1"

This became a favorite exercise that Reggie and Jodie would do at the end of each day. They found the exercise to be particularly helpful when one of them was feeling stuck, disconnected, or having a difficult time communicating their feelings, needs, or desires.

Jodie and Reggie invite you and your partner to give it a try for 21 days and notice the shifts within your relationship!

"3 Things, Plus 1"

Ideally, partners sit across from each other and look into each other's eyes throughout the exercise. More often than not, Reggie and Jodie performed the exercise lying in bed once the house was finally quiet and the lights had been turned off at the end of a long day.

Each partner gets a turn.

Whoever goes first starts by speaking aloud "3 Things" they particularly loved/liked about their partner THAT day:

- "One thing I love about you TODAY is _____."
- "The second thing I love about you TODAY is _____."
- "The third thing I love about you TODAY is _____."

These "things" can be *anything* you enjoyed about your partner that day: "You cooked dinner," "You arrived home safe," or, if it's been a particularly rough day, "You're still breathing."

Once the "3 Things" have been spoken aloud, it is time for the "Plus 1" of the day. The "Plus 1" is something that you really wish your partner had done/would do differently:

- "One thing you can do differently is _____."

The "Plus 1" can range from the seemingly mundane: "Remember to turn off the bathroom light when you're done," to the deeply meaningful – "Say you're sorry when you've hurt my feelings."

Now it is the second partner's turn to speak aloud their "3 Things, Plus 1." The exercise is completed with a physical embrace —just a hug and nothing more. The goal is to embrace each other for a full 30 seconds.

This exercise is similar to gratitude listing. It invites the brain to actively search for all the good that *already* exists within a relationship and to not only *see* the good that exists but to actively *verbalize* it to each other.

Oftentimes, it's easier to note all the things your partner *isn't* doing or all the ways they are falling short. When you allow yourself to focus, in real-time, on what you love about your partner, you begin to notice just how much you actually care for each other.

Once you've verbally expressed the three positive things to each other, it gently creates space to talk to each other about something that is troubling you, something you wish they'd stop doing or would begin to do differently.

The hug at the end seals the exercise with physical touch and connection, which is something that we as humans are constantly craving, and since it's just a hug, it helps release any expectations or sexual charge from the exercise.

Watch as Reggie and Jodie demo the "3 Things, Plus 1" exercise. Check out this exclusive bonus feature here!

SCAN THE QR CODE:

LUCY IN THE SKY, LILY IN THE FIELD

Jodie: We returned to D.C. and moved back into our house in Northern Virginia, which we had rented out while we were stationed in Florida. We got the kids back into the public school system that I really liked. I felt like I could breathe again. As I fully settled into my happy place, I started realizing that I wanted more.
Reggie: More of *me*?
Jodie: [hee-hee] Well, no, not exactly. I wanted more from *life*, and part of that was deciding that I wanted another baby.
Reggie: Ha! So you *did* want more of me!
Jodie: [sighs] I knew you'd see it like that.
Reggie: [laughs] How else can I see it?
Jodie: The truth is, I actually started thinking about having another baby while we were still in Jacksonville.
Reggie: But you didn't say anything to me about it until we settled back in D.C.
Jodie: No! I knew I couldn't tell you, not while we were

still in the craziness of our Navy life in Jacksonville. Honestly, when the idea first came to me, I thought I had lost my mind.

Reggie: I'd be okay with that.

Jodie: But then I realized that the idea of having another baby wasn't coming from my mind; it was coming from my heart. So there wasn't going to be much—if any—"logic" behind it. Still, I forced myself to wait a LONG time before I said anything to you.

Reggie: I think you should have told me from the very beginning.

Jodie: Nope, you would have attempted to cloud my judgment, and I needed to decide wholly and completely by myself, for myself. I know you don't want to hear this, but deciding whether I wanted to have another child wasn't about you.

Reggie: How can you possibly say that when I am the key component to you having another baby? How can you say that it wasn't about *me*?

Jodie: [laughs] Because it wasn't. It was about *me* and whether *I* still had more to give, if *I* could willingly bring another little life into this big world with all of its many challenges, and if *I* would still be able to give them and our other children my all.

Reggie: Okay, okay, but can I tell my story now?

Jodie: [laughs] You LOVE telling this story!

Reggie: Well, if it were the only time in your life that you were right, you would love telling this story, too.

———

A few years after having Rosie, Jodie told me that she was done having children. She said to me, "You need to get 'the mod.'" By "the mod," I'm referring to a vasectomy. The whole "permanent thing" was where I kind of had issues. This situation was one of the two times I've been right in our marriage. The first time was when I said, "Yep, Jodie's the one." The second time was when Jodie told me to get the mod, and I said, "You're gonna want one more." For many years—about eight or nine—we had this discussion at least once a year, sometimes more. Jodie would say, "Let's go ahead and get this done," and I would say, "Nope, you're gonna change your mind."

Jodie: [laughs] What can I say? I changed my mind.
Reggie: You have a track record of doing that with big life decisions.
Jodie: I do. I reserve the right to change my mind at any moment. The perceived magnitude of the situation really doesn't matter. If I feel deeply that something needs to change– I do it.
Reggie: Well, this time, it took a little longer than a weekend to change your mind, but it did happen. I'll always remember the day when you rolled over in bed, looked at me, and said, "I want to have one more." I just threw my hands up to the sky and said, "Yes! I knew it!" then quickly added, "Can we get started now?"
Jodie: [chuckles] You were *very* happy, and we did get started right away.
Reggie: My favorite part.
Jodie: [laughs] I like that part too! Just like the previous times, we got pregnant very quickly. When the pregnancy test came back positive, a part of me still couldn't believe

we were actually doing this. It seemed so crazy, but it also felt *so* right. Until it all went so wrong...

In the summer of 2008, they settled back in D.C., and Reggie went back to the daily grind at the Pentagon, working long hours from 6:00 a.m. to 8:00 p.m. Still, weekends were free, and there weren't any scheduled deployments or extended time away from home. Although grueling, the Pentagon job provided a predictable schedule. Being able to move back to their home and enroll the kids into a familiar school system allowed them to settle in quickly. Life was always going to be busy, but it seemed like the "right" time to have another baby.

The pregnancy got off to a good start, but early blood tests showed some concerns. Even though Rosie had faced so many medical challenges during her first few years of life, there was nothing that alerted them to this during pregnancy. All of Rosie's test results, even the newborn Apgar score, were perfect. Reggie and Jodie had undergone extensive genetic testing since Rosie was born in an attempt to diagnose her and screen for any potential family concerns. Over the course of many years, all those tests came back negative. There had never been any signs of possible problems with future pregnancies. So when the test results with their fourth pregnancy indicated that this wasn't going to be a typical pregnancy for Jodie, they were really taken aback.

Jodie: It was so disorienting.
Reggie: It really was.
Jodie: Foolishly, I remember thinking, *We already have a*

child with so many challenges. Surely, we've checked off that box. We'll get a pass with this baby because everything will be okay.

Reggie: But that wasn't the case.

Jodie: No, it wasn't. It didn't quite work like that.

Reggie: Toward the end of the second trimester, we lost the baby. Our sweet Lucy girl made it to heaven before she ever made it here.

Jodie: She is with us every day in the most amazing ways. Still, it was the hardest thing I have—*we have*—ever gone through.

Reggie: There were indicators pointing in that direction throughout the pregnancy, but nothing can ever prepare you for the loss of a child.

It's a quiet grief, the loss of an unborn child. No matter the road leading up to that loss. No matter how it occurred or if the loss was during the first, second, or third trimester. Miscarriages remain an unspoken grief. I wish Reggie and I, and society in general, talked about this more openly. So many women have experienced this type of loss, yet most of us feel completely alone when we do.

As a mother, you are led to believe that your only job while pregnant is to safely deliver your baby. There is so much pressure on a pregnant woman to do everything "right," from what we should eat, how we exercise and sleep, and our workload and the amount of stress we experience. When test results come back with concerns or the baby doesn't make it to full term, there's a tendency to feel like it's our fault. Many women feel like there was something they could or should have done differently to ensure that their baby arrived in this world safely and healthy.

Even though it didn't make logical sense, I felt like I was to blame. I was so confused because I wanted this baby so badly. I had always wanted a fourth baby. I just knew there was a little soul out there wanting to be a part of our family. I had spent so long deciding on the "right" time and determining if I was ready. I had been through so much heartache with the health concerns with my last child; I surely deserved a trouble-free pregnancy and healthy baby. And then to have had her and lose her before I even got to hold her... I understand now that this loss had nothing to do with "deserving," but at the time, I felt so lost and confused.

I was devastated. The grief ran so deep. The loss pulled me down in ways I had never experienced. The mourning was all-encompassing, much more intense than I anticipated. My grieving process took on a life of its own. I realize now that I was grieving a lot of things. It wasn't just the loss of our unborn baby, Lucy, but also the trauma I'd experienced with Rosie. One of the main differences was that this grief left me feeling hopeless. I never felt hopeless with Rosie, but this grief was very different. It felt like all that was possible had been taken from me. The loss of Lucy became a whole new challenge for Reggie and me to navigate.

Jodie: My friends still talk about that phone call when you told them about Lucy.
Reggie: Oh yeah, that was rough.
Jodie: I couldn't do it. We really hadn't broadcasted the news that I was even pregnant because I was having such a difficult pregnancy. Only our closest friends and family knew about it.
Reggie: These were our lifelong friends—the couples who

had been through so much with us during those early years with Rosie.

Jodie: Our ride-or-dies.

Reggie: I remember wishing, hoping, praying that my buddies would pick up the phone so I could just tell them, and then they would have to tell their wives, your besties. Alas, every time I made the call, one of your friends picked up the phone.

Jodie: That was when we all still had house phones. You wouldn't have that same trouble today. But do you know what they told me about that phone call?

Reggie: No idea.

Jodie: Well, aside from the shock and sadness of the call, they often remarked on *how* you told them.

Reggie: What do you mean?

Jodie: They were really touched when you said, "*We* lost the baby," not, "*Jodie* lost the baby."

Reggie: We had been together for over twenty years at this point.

Jodie: It felt like we'd experienced it all, but this loss was just so hard. It stretched us and pulled us in ways I never want to be stretched or pulled again.

Reggie: Once again, we were given the opportunity to deal with grief and loss as a couple.

Jodie: And, once again, we struggled. You reverted back to compartmentalizing and always focusing on the positive.

Reggie: Hey, it works!

Jodie: [laughs] Does it, though? I was depressed. I was incapable of compartmentalizing and having a positive outlook.

Reggie: Yeah, my method doesn't quite work the same for you.

Jodie: Avoidance is never the healthy option. Do you remember, months and months after we'd lost Lucy, what you said to me whenever I was feeling down?
Reggie: "What's wrong?"
Jodie: Oh my God! That drove me crazy! It was like you had *no idea* why I was sad, and you needed me to re-explain it to you *every* time.
Reggie: I just wanted you to be happy.
Jodie: [sighs] But I was sad. I needed to be sad. I wasn't interested in being happy.
Reggie: But why would you want to be sad? Nobody wants to be sad.
Jodie:[laughs]I did. I wanted and needed to experience this loss. Plus, it's not your job to *make* me happy.
Reggie: [laughing] I think it is.
Jodie: [laughs]And how's that working out for you?
Reggie: Somehow, things in our lives seem to work better when *you* make yourself happy.
Jodie: Bingo! I needed to go through the sadness before I could ever get to the happy.
Reggie: I just wanted to help you focus on and appreciate everything we had—three amazing children, us, and everything that we had created together.
Jodie: And for a long time, I wasn't ready to go there. I also started feeling like I needed to grieve *for* you—since, in my humble opinion, you were doing a *really* terrible job at it—which, in hindsight, was a *really* bad idea on my part.

I am not someone who likes to share my negative emotions or burdens with anyone. I have always liked to be alone as I deal with my emotions. *In the simplest terms, I am not a talker when it comes to expressing and dealing with challenging emotions. I feel like it's a burden that I don't want to place on Jodie. She doesn't need to deal with that. She's got enough shit to deal with. I would process everything on my own, usually staying up late until 2:00 or 3:00 in the morning. There were countless times when Jodie would ask, "What time did you come to bed? Why did you stay up so late?" I would process my grief while watching* The Godfather *or* Kill Bill *for the ten thousandth time.*

One night, I was watching The Equalizer *when Jodie had had enough and was really upset. I finally confessed what was really going on. At that moment, I realized I was placing a burden on our relationship by* not *sharing how I was dealing with my emotional grief. I learned that Jodie and I grieved in different ways. The key to staying connected was through clear, open communication.*

Once again, Jodie and Reggie had to learn how to deal with their own grieving process and recognize that they both handled grief in different ways. It was an ongoing and continuous process. They were on a journey to get to a better place with each other, but life kept throwing obstacles in their path. One of the biggest lessons they learned was that there was no right or wrong way to grieve. Giving each other space and grace, especially when grieving, is a lifelong process, and it proved to be beneficial to their relationship. Jodie understood that when Reggie stayed up late watching TV by himself, he was actually processing his grief in his own time and space. Reggie stopped asking Jodie, *"What's wrong?"* and would simply hold her or let her be sad without trying to fix it. Sometimes, it only takes simple awareness and simple actions to create cosmic shifts.

THE COURAGE TO TRY AGAIN

Reggie: The good part was it took you less time to decide you wanted to try again.

Jodie: It took me about a year or so. Even though I was still grieving the loss of Lucy, I was still feeling that another little soul was out there, ready to complete our family. It turned out that Lily was meant to be the final member of our family.

Reggie: It was Lily, and we just can't imagine this world without Lily in it.

Jodie: She's our rainbow baby.

Reggie: I guess this was how it was supposed to be because I was able to talk you into one more. I don't think I could have talked you into two more.

Jodie: [laughs] No, there was never going to be five—not on purpose, at least.

Reggie: But we ended up having five children, just not as one might expect.

I was super scared during my fifth pregnancy in ways I never had been before. I was too aware of everything that could go wrong during pregnancy. At this time in 2010, I was thirty-six years old, an "advanced maternal" age, when there were no guarantees that this baby would make it to term. It was a really challenging time. I tried to focus on that feeling—that internal knowing that lived deep down inside of me, the one that had been niggling at me for years that we were meant to have another baby.

Thankfully, my pregnancy went according to plan, and we had another beautiful baby girl. Lily, our fifth baby—but the fourth one physically—had restored my faith in so many things. She was a magical ray of light, packed with a punch from the moment she arrived. When you have a typically developing child born after having one with significant special needs, EVERYTHING becomes miraculous! I marveled at ALL of Lily's milestones: sitting up, self-feeding, walking, talking, running! Wow! Look at all she can do! I realized that I had taken "basic" milestones for granted with our first two. After having a child who never hit a single developmental milestone, it was truly a delight to watch Lily grow and develop with ease! Every little thing, like holding a Cheerio and then successfully eating it, was utterly ah-MAZing!

Reggie: There were so many mundane things we took for granted with our two "healthy" children.
Jodie: It was hard not to. We didn't know anything else. We didn't know how challenging sitting up could be or that one of our children might never read or be able to live an independent life.
Reggie: After everything we'd experienced with Rosie, watching Lily grow according to plan filled us with a whole new level of awe and amazement.
Jodie: In some ways, we were like first-time parents all over again, even though there is a seventeen-year gap between our first and last baby.
Reggie: That was another benefit of having Lily so much later in life. She taught her older sister, Olivia, who was

almost ready for college, what life would look like if she had a baby before she was ready.

Jodie: [laughs] Olivia took care of her baby sister quite a bit. Plus, she watched my body go through all stages of pregnancy and postpartum, which can't help but leave a lasting impression when you're a junior in high school.

One of the things I loved about living in our suburban world outside of D.C., or "Pleasantville," as Reggie called it, was that I knew all my neighbors. Whenever someone new moved in, we would drop off a plant or baked goods to welcome them to the neighborhood.

A new neighbor moved in when Lily was six months old. I had baked some brownies, so Olivia, who was seventeen at the time, was going to join me in meeting the new neighbors. I grabbed the brownies and handed the baby to Olivia, then the three of us headed just a few doors down. Just as I was about to ring the bell, Olivia looked at me and sighed. "Mom, can we switch?"

"Sure, but why?" I asked as she handed me the baby, and I gave her the brownies.

"This is the first time they're meeting me, and I don't want them to assume the baby is mine," Olivia said.

Over the next few years, we faced this assumption over and over again. Everyone assumed Olivia was Lily's mom. When Lily was older, around two or three, people would ask her, "Is that your mom?" referring to Olivia. Lily would be so appalled by the question. She never understood how anyone could think her sister was her mother, and she had no problem letting them know how crazy they were for even thinking it.

Reggie: It is an interesting perspective, having children seventeen years apart.

Jodie: Yeah, and people seem to have zero qualms about asking, especially with our older kids, if they all have the same mom and dad.

Reggie: Yep, it's the same for all of them.

Jodie: [giggles] As far as *you* know it is!

Reggie: Well, I do wake up to a different person every day.

Jodie: That's what you like to tell me.

Reggie: Because it's true. But the perspective of having a child seventeen years younger than the first one brings...

Jodie: All the things that you used to stress and worry about became a lot less worrisome. It's so much easier to know your child is actually gonna be okay. They're gonna read on their own time, learn all their math facts, and make friends. It's all gonna work out. You can just relax and let go more.

Reggie: You also realize the really big stuff, like college decisions, driving, traveling, and living on their own, are yet to come, so be sure to fully enjoy the early years. It gave us a vast and appreciative perspective.

A CROSSROADS

After having Lily, Jodie realized that her family was now complete. She also began to realize that she was ready to focus on herself and her own personal goals. After spending more than twenty years focusing solely on the family, their navy life, and marriage, Jodie felt a strong calling to expand her gifts and talents *outside* of the home. Jodie first found her way to personal development and the world of entrepreneurship. She started a successful business in the health and wellness industry.

Along with fostering and leading a team of fellow entrepreneurs, she enjoyed forging deeper roots within her community. From there, she moved into the world of energy healing and became a Reiki Master Teacher. Her business of guiding and assisting others with their own personal healing through Reiki and energy work flourished and firmly established her life outside of the Navy. At the same time, Reggie was being pulled deeper into his Navy career, and he felt that he still had more to contribute. But a significant crossroads lay ahead.

———

Reggie: The Navy offered me a new position: Major Command.
Jodie: That is kinda a big deal, one that not many people in the military ever achieve.
Reggie: Yeah, it was a big job. It was like my previous command job but on steroids, with more responsibilities and even more people working for me. Actually, it's *with* me because I never feel anyone works *for* me. One of my fundamental life tenets is that the key to success is that we work together... so not *for* but *with*.
Jodie: A fabulous achievement in your career, however...
Reggie: Taking the job would require us to move again.
Jodie: This was around the time I put my stake in the ground. At this point, I had given the Navy twenty years. I was personally done with all the upheaval it had caused, and I didn't want to uproot the family and move the kids *again*.
Reggie: Right.

Jodie: I mean, I was fully ready to support you and your career achievements. I was just going to do it from my couch in our suburbia home, not through yet another move or by attending a million other military functions. So, we decided to seriously look at the "unaccompanied option."

Reggie: I had the option of taking the Major Command position, but it would be in a location where the family couldn't join me.

Jodie: A far-off location indeed... Bahrain, to be exact.

FINAL THOUGHTS

Dealing with loss is always challenging in a relationship, especially when each person deals with grief differently. Jodie and Reggie learned the art of communication over the course of their decades-long relationship, but losing an unborn child forced them to learn a new language of understanding and trust. They had both grieved for the loss of Rosie in their own ways, but the loss of Lucy introduced another dynamic they had never faced before. It allowed them a deeper understanding of how they processed and moved through challenging situations. It brought greater insight into communicating in a way so they both felt heard and understood.

KEY TAKEAWAY

There is no right or wrong way to grieve. Giving each other space and grace, especially when grieving, is a lifelong process, so always be gentle with yourself and your partner.

WHAT THEY WISH THEY HAD KNOWN: THE POWER AND (NECESSITY) OF SURRENDER

When life brings heartaches and challenges to your doorstep, trusting and allowing yourself to surrender to the flow of life, rather than resisting or attempting to force change, is the most powerful and peaceful way to move through the upheaval.

When Jodie and Reggie unexpectedly lost their 4th baby, Lucy, they hadn't yet made their way to *The Surrender Experiment* by Michale Singer. *The Surrender Experiment* offers a powerful reminder that by letting go of control, we begin to align with the natural flow of the universe. Furthermore, it is the *resistance* to whatever life brings our way that is the actual cause of our greatest suffering. Surrendering to the flow of life allows harmony, growth, and peace within.

Surrender doesn't mean we won't grieve or experience loss, but it does remind us that we *can* trust in the flow of life and that everything will *always* work out for our greatest good. Through the act of surrender and bravely letting go, we actively open ourselves to possibilities far greater than we could ever imagine or possibly orchestrate. The goodness of life will always show itself —as long as we allow it to do so. Surrendering, rather than attempting to dictate and control life based on our personal preferences, allows us to remain open to all the wondrous possibilities that are way beyond our own limited experience and human capabilities. The power of surrender can also be brought into your relationship. Ultimately, surrendering to the flow of life invites us to stay present and release unrealistic expectations, which allows love and connection to strengthen and grow.

BAHRAIN AND BEYOND

Reggie: Just the other day, I was talking to this guy who committed to moving across the country for a job. He accepted the position, which was a great opportunity. He and his family packed up their stuff, and as they were about to drive away, his wife told him she couldn't make the move.
Jodie: Yikes.
Reggie: She told him, "You can go, but the baby and I are staying here."
Jodie: She changed her mind. It happens to the best of us. Plus, I think there's something else going on there.
Reggie: No kidding, but I just...
Jodie: Hey, we reserve the right to change our minds—always. I feel like we've covered this a few times already.
Reggie: [laughs]Well, yes, but I feel like the last-minute decision could have been avoided. It created turmoil for lots of people, not just for this guy and his wife.
Jodie: Possibly. I think it comes back to open communica-

tion with your partner and also knowing what you want. Sometimes, it's hard to know what you want until the wheels are in motion. At least, for me, that's often the case. Then I'm suddenly like, "Oh crap! I *can't* do this."

Reggie: I just couldn't help but feel that our story could've somehow helped that couple. Major life decisions shouldn't have to come down to the literal last minute.

Jodie: I agree. A frank and open conversation could have happened long before the decision, but it's tough to do that sometimes. It takes work to openly communicate with each other.

Reggie: It does. I doubt those feelings of not wanting to go appeared at the last second.

Jodie: Oh no, they've been there, but maybe she thought she could take one for the team. I know what that's like; I've had that mindset many times. But then she realized she couldn't go and said something about it at the last minute. I applaud her for following her heart. Better late than never, right? Believe me; there were many times back in the day when I wished I had known what I wanted and actually spoke up more.

Deciding whether Reggie would take the job and move to Bahrain was a conversation they discussed time and again. They played out all the possible outcomes, weighing the pros and cons and making lists, all to decide what was best for them and their family. The dilemma was layered. Reggie still felt like he had more to accomplish in his military career. There were concerns about where the kids were in their lives—high school wasn't the best time to move, and then there were Rosie's medical needs and special education. Then there was the question of whether or not Jodie was up for another move and another tour. She wasn't.

Throughout Reggie's career, especially after he'd been in command of a squadron in Jacksonville, there were multiple occasions when people of color thanked him and expressed appreciation that someone who looked like them could succeed in the military. The lack of diversity in the military was a real challenge, and as one of the few minority senior officers in the Navy, Reggie felt a responsibility to continue to be an example of success, inspiring others to pursue a career in the Navy. However, he struggled with that responsibility and balancing his career with the constant sacrifice for his family.

Young sailors were always coming up to me to say thank you. One conversation stands out to me. I was standing in the entranceway of the aviation command center in Jacksonville, where the pictures of all of the leaders of the U.S. government, Navy, and, in particular, my aviation community were on display. As I looked at the photos, a young sailor came up to me and asked.

"Sir, why should I stay in the Navy when my chance of success is so small?" He pointed to the photos. "Look at that wall of photos. There's no one up there who looks like me. I know you made it to command, but I'm not you. I don't have your skills or charisma. People don't like me, so I just don't see how I make it to be a commander."

I looked the sailor in the eye and said, "If I can do it, you sure as hell can do it. I was not half the sailor you are when I was your age. You don't have to be me to succeed. Just be true to yourself, and you will achieve great things."

That sailor thanked me, and I saw the renewed confidence in his eyes. I continued to mentor him over the next few years, and I was not surprised when he was eventually selected to command a squadron.

To further his career, Reggie decided that the best option was to take unaccompanied orders overseas to Bahrain for a year. He had done six- and eight-month deployments in the past, so he and Jodie felt confident that they could handle a year of separation. Plus, the Navy could not provide Rosie full medical support in that environment if they moved. Thus, a year apart became the preferred choice instead of uprooting the entire family. In the fall of 2011, Reggie would move to the Middle East while Jodie remained in Virginia with the children.

It was a long year with many challenges. Even though newer technology was available, letter writing was still the tried-and-true way of communication for Jodie and Reggie. The increased connectivity options did make a huge difference, especially for the kids. Being able to "see" their father when they went to school or before bed was *mostly* helpful, though this also created unique obstacles.

So I was sitting in an African country, making my way on commercial airlines from Manama, Bahrain, to Djibouti on the African continent. I was literally riding on planes with goats and chickens. In the airport, when I had an eight-hour layover, I called Jodie on a public phone to check in. She told me there was an emergency at the house: the water heater imploded. As I tried to help her resolve the issue, the line went dead. I searched the entire airport for another phone, weaving around hundreds of people who were sleeping in every open space of this "new" airport. With every minute that passed, I was getting more and more frustrated. I then received a call on my work phone that one of our aircraft flying in Djibouti had almost been in a mid-air collision. When I finally found a public phone to call Jodie back, I simultaneously reviewed the procedures and notifications with my Navy team about the aircraft-related incident. This tour was filled with many moments of competing priorities from both home and work..

Reggie: It was challenging because, in the past, before so much connectivity, it would take weeks before I would even hear about an issue.

Jodie: And most of the time, it was resolved before you were even aware of it.

Reggie: Right, but now I was hearing about it in real-time.

Jodie: It's tough because you felt like you could be there, but in reality, you couldn't. You were on the other side of the world with your hands tied behind your back. You could talk me through stuff, but you couldn't actively do things.

Reggie: It was an additional challenge, one that we hadn't anticipated because we thought email and Skype would only make things easier. It was definitely a dual-sided conversation.

Jodie: And you were so far away. There was no hopping on a plane to come home if you needed to. Even in an emergency, it was going to take you a couple of days to get to us.

Reggie: It created a whole new shift in perspective.

Jodie: More access and total connectivity isn't always better.

Reggie: Amen. However, it brought that awareness home. It was tough, but it was really interesting to see the silver linings that came from my time away.

―――

Reggie and our son, Grant, were very close. He had coached Grant for many years in soccer and basketball. Reggie also took Grant to practices or games, especially when they were too far away or too difficult to manage, with both Rosie and Lily in tow. When Reggie left for the year in the Middle East, Grant really felt his father's absence. In addition to that, his big sister Olivia, who took on much of the household workload, went off to her first year in college. It was an abrupt start to Grant's freshman year of high school. I also felt the absence of Reggie and Olivia acutely. Reggie had never been gone for an entire year, and as if that wasn't hard enough, I had to drop off my firstborn at college and navigate life without her daily presence. I knew Grant was feeling their absence, so I carved out time for us to spend together. We got into a good routine of putting "the girlies" to bed and then watching whatever shows he wanted to watch. We became big fans of The Big Bang Theory and spent our evenings together laughing. Grant grew up a lot that year, and I was really proud of him.

Jodie: Admit it, you were a little jelly when you came back, and Grant and I had grown so close.
Reggie: And it's still that way... I haven't gotten him back.
Jodie: What do you mean? You guys are still close! You just wanted him all to yourself. You like to do that with all our children.
Reggie: [laughs] Me? I'm not the one who hogs the children.
Jodie: I can't help it. I love hanging out with our children, and they love hanging out with me!
Reggie: Anyway, let's get back on topic. Your personal growth journey was another silver lining. You really kicked it into high gear during this time.
Jodie: I started to find that I had more bandwidth, which was kind of the opposite of what you would expect with you gone. I felt like I had lots more time on my hands.

Reggie: Are you trying to say I take up too much of your time?

Jodie: [laughs] Never "too much," just "a lot" of it! But being back in our home, with the kids in the same school system and Rosie seeing the same doctors and therapists, everything was running smoothly, so I was able to settle in quickly. I found myself wondering what was next for me. What would I like to do with my time?

I discovered this desire for greater depth and satisfaction, not only for myself, but for our relationship and in life in general. I felt this pull—as if I had more to learn and more to give. I was giving so much of myself to home, in relationships, and as a mother, but I felt there were other ways I could use my gifts and talents, even though I didn't know exactly what it would look like. That was when I dove into personal development and healing. I read A LOT of books. I found my way to reiki and energy work, along with mindset work, personality, and archetypal explorations. I became obsessed with Enneagram, natal astrology, and Human Design and took courses on all of them—I couldn't get enough! I started using my newfound knowledge, not only for myself, but also in our relationship. Reggie was always a willing participant in whatever I was working on or learning about. He saw the benefits of my own healing process and, therefore, felt more comfortable with me bringing these tools into our relationship.

Jodie: One of the things I've always appreciated is that you've always been so open to any exploration.

Reggie: I try.

Jodie: And even though, at that time, you really needed to focus on the job you were doing in Command, overseeing thousands of people at the tip of the spear...

Reggie: Over multiple continents.

Jodie: Through all that, you always prioritized me and my interests back home. Even if you weren't sure where it was leading or what I was doing, there was always an unyielding level of support. You never told me not to do something or tried to pull me back.

Reggie: I never said, "Haven't you got enough on your plate?"

Jodie: Ha! No, I would *not* have liked that. Now that I know I'm a Manifesting Generator in Human Design,[i] which is akin to saying I'm a multi-passionate being constantly pivoting to new things. It really makes sense that I always have so many plates spinning at the same time.

Reggie: But we didn't know any of that mumbo jumbo yet.

Jodie: We had no idea!

Reggie: I think it was all part of respecting each other. Plus, I've always been interested in your growth as an individual.

Jodie: I feel that.

Reggie: It's something I've tried to do from the very beginning. I still ask myself regularly: What do I need to do so Jodie always *feels* my support?

Jodie: You are really good at that. You're even getting better with it the longer we do this.

Reggie: Thank you. I've realized it doesn't really matter if I totally agree. [chuckles] What matters is how much I can support you in doing whatever it is that *you* feel like you need to do. I've always felt that type of support from you throughout my military career. So I see it as part of our continued growth as a couple and as a team, thinking about each other in that way.

When one person in the relationship starts focusing on personal growth and self-healing, they naturally begin to move in a new direction. When they explore new ventures, ideas, and possibilities, their partner will notice that something is different, even if they aren't sure what it is. It might not even be at a conscious level, but they will sense that something has shifted in their partner. When this positive shift brings greater peace, joy, and possibilities into their lives, these changes are difficult to ignore. Oftentimes, this shift creates unexpected tension within the relationship. The partner doing the work of healing and letting go will literally vibrate at a different frequency. If the couple had felt "in sync" before, like Reggie and Jodie did for the most part, this new frequency can feel quite uncomfortable and is very noticeable. If the partner hasn't begun their own journey of healing or mindset work, they may feel like they are being left behind. They might not be ready to begin their own personal growth journey, but the tension won't release. One of the last things anyone wants to experience in a relationship is the fear of being left behind or that their partner might outgrow them.

Jodie: We started to feel some of that tension. It wasn't always a bad thing, or at least I didn't think so.
Reggie: I didn't care much for it.

Jodie: [laughs] Was it a classic case of "if you can't beat 'em, join 'em?"

Reggie: Kinda. But while you were exploring all these new horizons, I still needed to focus on the job, the work that was right in front of me.

Jodie: You did have a lot on your plate, attempting to keep the world safe for democracy and all.

Reggie: [laughs] Exactly. As supportive as I tried to be, I still felt like, *Wow, I'm kind of out of this. I'm not sure exactly where it's going.*

Jodie: I wanted you to come with me, but at the same time, it got to the point where I wasn't stopping for anyone or anything. For the first time in over twenty-five years, I started to get a little selfish. Now, I know it's a "healthy selfishness," but at the time, it felt very uncomfortable.

Reggie: But you kept going.

Jodie: I had to because something was pulling me along.

Reggie: And you were eager to follow.

Jodie: I was.

Reggie: We've all heard it time and again that when a relationship ends, the couple will often say, "We just grew apart."

Jodie: And you were NOT going to let that be the case for us.

Reggie: Nope.

Jodie: I'm so glad you weren't.

Reggie: Part of what we came to realize was that a military career wasn't conducive to the type of growth and exploration we were looking to do as a couple.

Jodie: It came to a point when we asked ourselves, "How do *we* want to move forward?"

Reggie: We knew we wanted to be together, but we started to realize...
Jodie: After almost twenty-eight years of service...
Reggie: That maybe it was time to retire from the Navy.
Jodie: We'd done enough separations, enough moves, enough prioritizing others. It was time for me and you.
Reggie: I agreed, but I still felt like I had more to give. I'd done well enough in all my job roles and was in the running for that next big thing. I didn't know if I wanted to give that up. So how could we do both? This became the ultimate compromise: "Okay, we're going to continue down this Navy path, but we're going to set parameters, and if things don't happen in a certain way within a timeframe, then we're done."
Jodie: We finally created healthy boundaries with the Navy and your career—boundaries that we felt comfortable with as a couple and for our family.

RETIREMENT

The next major achievement in my naval career was my consideration for selection as an admiral. I was ready to retire, and Jodie was more than ready, but I kept thinking about the young sailors who had reminded me how much it inspired them to see someone who looked like them succeed. It filled me with a sense of responsibility to continue being that example of success for them. I was also keenly aware of the toll my career was having on my family. In the end, Jodie and I came to a compromise: We would give the Navy one chance to select me.

The selection process for an admiral can happen on the first window of opportunity, your fifth, or it may never happen at all. We decided that if the Navy truly saw my value, they would select me at the first opportunity. But if they didn't, then I would retire. At this point, Jodie and I were going to take control of our timeline and not let the Navy determine it.

In the end, I wasn't selected at the first opportunity. There were many people on my leadership team who told me to stay and keep going because it wasn't a matter of *if* but *when* I would be selected. While those words were encouraging, there was still no guarantee that I would be selected for admiral, and Jodie and I were ready to move forward. The Navy had made it clear that they didn't love me as much as they professed, so it made the decision to move on much easier. I feel we manifested the "no" decision because, in my heart of hearts, I knew it was time to live my life with only one top priority: my family. Jodie and I were ready to continue exploring ourselves as a couple and take it to the next level. After twenty-eight years of dedicating ourselves to military service, our journey was complete.

Reggie: Once again, we learned that we have to take the time to reconnect—like our trip to Paris—if we're feeling disconnected.
Jodie: It requires us *making* the time.
Reggie: Even with four kids and all their schedules and all their needs.
Jodie: And with both our jobs and our individual interests.
Reggie: We still have to make time for *just us*.
Jodie: Period.
Reggie: We also don't live in a world of ultimatums. We've never taken the "my way or the highway" approach. Instead, we approach life as: I want this, you want this. How do we make this work the best?

Jodie: When one of us feels really strongly about something, we allow them to steer the ship and take things in the direction they desire.

Reggie: There has to be enough trust to say, "Okay, I'm open, so let's give this a try."

Jodie: [laughs] It can be hard to release control and just trust... for some of us in particular!

Reggie: I don't know what you're talking about.

Jodie: We are both highly intuitive people with Sacral (guttural) Authority,[ii] so when one of us "feels" something at an instinctual level, then we know it's the way to go.

Reggie: It hasn't steered us wrong.

Jodie: Nope, it hasn't. We just have to learn to listen to it and trust to take action in that direction. We have to trust that the universe has our back and that life is always working for our greatest good—sometimes, we just have to get out of the way.

Reggie: I can look back on that time now and realize that if we stayed in the Navy longer, I don't know if we would be in as good a place as we are today.

Jodie: I know. And no, we wouldn't.

FINAL THOUGHTS

There is little doubt that staying in the Navy any longer would have created more challenges for their relationship. Whereas, honoring the boundaries they had created as a couple opened the door to many new possibilities. It allowed them to get to a point in their lives where they were able to prioritize their connection with each other. Jodie's vision for her and Reggie as a couple started to lead the way. Greater abundance, more adventures, increased joy, and love of life were all on the horizon.

Moving into the next chapter of their lives opened up many new and exciting experiences. The greatest lesson from this phase was learning how to grow together. Jodie and Reggie found even more ways to make shared memories that didn't involve their kids or work. This allowed them to be a couple in every sense of the word and have adventures together.

Many couples who spend years together start to live separate lives. Usually, this is not a conscious decision; it just seems to happen as competing priorities take each person in a different direction. Before they know it, they are making a lot of memories that don't involve their partner. One day, they'll wake up to find that not only do they really not know the person next to them, but they may not even be sure if they like them. This is the unintended consequence of making separate life memories.

KEY TAKEAWAY

As you move through life in a long-term relationship, find ways to make memories together. Finding ways to make shared memories keeps connectivity alive and helps prevent couples from growing apart.

WHAT THEY WISH THEY HAD KNOWN: HUMAN DESIGN ENERGY TYPE

Everything is Energy, and Energy is Everything!

Human Design(HD) is a self-discovery system that blends ancient wisdom and modern science to explain and expound personal energy. It provides an energetic blueprint for how we are each uniquely designed to navigate life. HD is a complete tool that offers practical insights into one's personality, decision-making process, strengths, and life purpose. While primarily a personal development tool, HD can be readily used in romantic relationships.

While it's essential, first and foremost, to learn and understand your own Human Design, once you do, HD is also a highly effective tool to access and enhance your partnership. Human Design invites you to navigate not only your energy, but also your partner's. It also allows for deeper insights into their personality and decision-making process, along with understanding the compatibility and possible challenges between energy types.

Jodie's Human Design Energy type is a Manifesting Generator (MG). Manifesting Generators are multi-passionate beings who pivot easily and readily. Her energy enjoys learning on the fly. She prefers to quickly move through projects, easily gleaning the insights she needs for mastery so she can just move on.

Reggie's Human Design energy type is a pure Generator. His energy is powerfully magnetic and always ON. Reggie is much more methodical and prefers a step-by-step approach when committing to a project. When he commits, he is ALL in and has little desire to shift or waiver until he feels satisfied.

Although Jodie and Reggie are different Energy Types, they also have similarities due to them both having Sacral Authorities, meaning they both do their best decision-making by listening to their gut feeling in the moment and following it. Also, they are similar in that they both thrive when they follow the strategy they share, which is "to respond," allowing life to present opportunities before taking action.

While they each have access to sustainable energy—due to their Sacral Authority—they handle projects and like to work differently. Jodie dives right in, rarely, if ever, follows directions, and jumps around while working on a project. Reggie, on the other hand, moves through methodically, always reads the instructions, and makes sure he has all the parts needed before starting a project. Reggie is very good at actually completing projects, whereas Jodie is ready to pivot to the next thing long before she's completed the last.

A practical application of how their energies work can together be seen when they take on household projects. Jodie's always leading the charge. She's ready to easily shift course as needed, while Reggie is fastidious and tirelessly comes behind her, completing the task and doing any necessary cleanup. These two energies, the MG and Generator, can sometimes be in conflict, but they can also complement each other when they understand what each energy is bringing to the project.

Learning how a Manifesting Generator and a Generator energetically work together helped Reggie and Jodie to understand not only themselves but also each other better. Together, they have learned that a Manifesting Generator's dynamic energy, along with a Generator's steady focus, are a recipe for a powerful, energetic partnership.

BAHRAIN AND BEYOND

To learn more about Human Design and how it informs their relationship, watch this exclusive live clip with Jodie and Reggie!

SCAN THE QR CODE:

THE AFTERLIFE

Retiring from the Navy after twenty-eight years of active-duty service opened a new world of possibilities for the couple. Reggie planned to continue working. He started his own consulting company and was in conversations with many companies. Jodie's work as a Reiki Master Teacher continued to grow and expand. She was feeling deeply satisfied with her work and had begun taking on clients from across the globe.

The couple planned to stay in Virginia, where they could safely put down some roots. After almost three decades of waiting on orders and wondering where they might be stationed next, they were finally able to take charge and make decisions based solely on their needs. Jodie had been ready for this moment for a long time and was eagerly leading the charge about what came next for the couple and their family.

Jodie: I felt like I was finally able to exhale.
Reggie: Twenty-eight years was a long time to be holding your breath.
Jodie: Yes, it was! It was so freeing to no longer live from one set of orders to the next. I could finally put down roots and focus on things like updating our kitchen.
Reggie: And the bathrooms, and the floors, and the roof...
Jodie: Yes, I had wanted to do major renovations on our house for years, but we never knew if we'd be staying or renting it out again.
Reggie: Now you went a little crazy.
Jodie: I got exactly what I wanted, and I was so happy with the outcome!
Reggie: See? It was worth the wait.
Jodie: I don't know about all that, but I do know that after you retired, I felt like it was my time to shine. I felt like I could explore more opportunities.
Reggie: You already had your reiki business going.
Jodie: I did, but after you retired, I could amp it all up. That was what I wanted to do, and I could finally count on you to be home!
Reggie: Um, I did start another job. I wasn't just hanging around the house.
Jodie: True, but it was a totally different vibe. You were home every night, and you didn't deploy. You rarely even traveled.
Reggie: It was a dramatic shift.
Jodie: And I was here for it! My favorite part might be that you finally learned how to "lunch."

When Reggie first retired from the Navy, he took a few months off before starting his job for corporate America. This gave us a new opportunity to spend some quality time with each other during the day. Over the years, Reggie was rarely home in the middle of the day. Now, he was home all day, every day. So, on a random Tuesday, I invited him out to lunch at a local spot that was popping every day of the week. As we sat down at our table, he seemed so distracted. He kept looking around with this confused look on his face. I asked him, "What's up?"

Incredulously, he said, "Who are all these people? And why aren't they at work?"

Laughing, I said, "Well, they're probably just on their lunch breaks. Not everyone spends their lunch break at their desk like you have for the past twenty-eight years."

He couldn't get over how many people were out enjoying a leisurely lunch on a weekday. Then he learned another valuable lesson: He ordered not one, not two, but three Moscow mules with his meal. When we got home, he passed out on the couch until well after the kids came home from school. When he woke up, I explained that having three beverages at lunch wasn't advisable, especially when your children need you after school. So, it took him a minute to learn how to "lunch" and still be productive for the rest of the day.

Reggie: There were *a lot* of people out there.
Jodie: It was just the normal amount of people, but you were so taken aback by the fact that they were lunching in the middle of the day.
Reggie: It's kind of inefficient.
Jodie: I think you felt left out. It was as if you realized everything you'd been missing all those years, eating your

homemade lunch at your desk or at the food court on base.

Reggie: I was getting shit done. There was no time for leisurely lunches.

Jodie: And now look at you! You're an old pro.

Reggie: I got the hang of it pretty quickly.

Jodie: But you don't have three Moscow mules at lunch anymore.

Reggie: [laughs] No, I don't.

The truth is that for many individuals, retiring after decades of naval service can be very challenging. After spending most of their lives in the military, transitioning to the civilian world can be an oddly rude awakening. The lack of camaraderie and service to others in the civilian world can be difficult. Thankfully, Jodie and Reggie had been preparing for the possibility of retirement for the previous three years. They honored the boundaries they created as a couple and were in the process of taking the next steps according to their plan. Once they got clear as a couple and decided how they wanted to move forward, all the other pieces fell into place.

Jodie: When the time came for you to retire from the Navy, you were *done*.

Reggie: Done and done.

Jodie: It was actually a really smooth transition. I think a lot of that was because we created clarity around what we wanted as a couple. We understood that moving on from

the Navy was by no means the end, but in many ways, it was a totally new beginning.
Reggie: Right. I never got tied up in the Navy or let it define who I was. To me, the Navy and my career were the tools I used to impact people's lives.
Jodie: *Positively* impact people's lives, which you definitely did.
Reggie: When I transitioned out from the Navy, the questions became: "How do I continue to help people? How can I continue to provide the type of impact that will make a difference?"
Jodie: That did become the challenge. You had spent twenty-eight years *serving* in the Navy, which is truly a career of service, so when you got out, you still had the desire to serve, but now you had to find a new avenue to be able to do so.

In addition to starting his own LLC, Reggie took a post-retirement job in the world of government contracting. He saw this as the next logical step after his naval career. He always considered his job in government contracting as a stepping stone—a transitional period until he could decide what he really wanted to do with his life.

The transition from being in uniform to civilian life was easy. I started my first "real" job of my life. For thirty-plus years, I didn't have a traditional job, but I was engaging in my calling, which was what my naval career provided. My new civilian job still had opportunities to impact people's lives, but that wasn't the sole purpose. Since I didn't find the same satisfaction in my civilian job as I found in my navy career, I sought new ways to contribute and make a difference in people's lives. I joined a few non-profit boards and used the experiences and skills I had acquired in the Navy to help those in my community.

Serving others is a big part of my identity and my life's purpose, so it was great to find new avenues to provide service. What's funny is that I initially treated my job in the defense industry like every other job I had in the Navy. For example, in the Navy, I worked until the job was done, even if that meant eighteen-hour days. That is not the mentality in the corporate world. They pay you to work forty hours a week—no more, no less. It wasn't until Jodie kept reminding me, while I was in my tenth- or eleventh-hour workday, that I was only being paid for eight hours. My boss was giving me grief for being at work so early and staying so late. Eventually, I realized that the only person pushing to get things done at that pace was me, and I needed to change my ways. It is much different when your job is your calling than if it is just a job. I had to learn how to work in the right way. That was the hardest adjustment.

Jodie: You are a natural-born leader with a heart for service. That is one of the reasons why the Navy was good for you.
Reggie: You think?
Jodie: I do. The thing you really loved most about being in the Navy was connecting with so many people and assisting them however you could to make a difference.
Reggie: That's true.
Jodie: That desire lives within you, and it didn't go away when you retired. It will never go away.

Reggie: It really didn't. It was challenging because I felt like there were so many other Navy lives that I could have positively affected.

Jodie: I can see that. But since you've retired, you've started to see the ripple effect. You've only begun to realize how many lives you have touched—many of which you never met—and how much of an impact your years of service have had on them.

Mentoring has always been my favorite way to give back. The opportunities to do so seem to come out of nowhere, which is quite interesting. One of my favorite stories was when I was traveling on the D.C. Metro to work. Instead of taking the Blue Line, which was my normal route, I decided to take the Yellow Line.

As I stepped onto the train, I thought, "I wonder who I'm gonna meet today." When I do something out of the norm, it seems like someone or something comes into my life. Sure enough, I met a young Navy man who was dealing with a bunch of issues and big life decisions. He had been in the same squadron I had once commanded and had seen my picture on the wall among all the other previous squadron commanders. He told me that he would walk by that picture, wanting to meet me one day. Lo and behold, while vacationing in D.C., he met me on the Metro. We exchanged information, and over the next couple of years, I mentored this young man and helped him eventually reach his goal of going to law school.

Another reason why I stayed in the Navy was because I wanted to be an advocate for people. Once I retired, I realized that I could still be an advocate because I had many friends in higher-level positions who could propose change when called upon.

A great example of this was a young man whom my old college roommate, Rich, connected me with. They had been on a flight together, and the young man told my friend that he had been hit by a drunk driver while going through flight school. After he came out of a coma, the doctors told him that he would never walk again. He was determined to get all his mobility back and become the pilot he had always dreamed of being. That was his mental state when he was going through rehab, and he would stop at nothing to reach his goals. He succeeded, overcoming every hurdle not only to walk again, but he was eventually cleared to fly. However, the physical requirements to be a naval aviator are very stringent, and the Navy system wasn't willing to clear him to fly naval aircraft.

My friend Rich connected me with the young man. After hearing his story, I did some research and discovered there was no reason, based on his current medical status, that he should not be allowed to fly. Unfortunately, the easy answer for the Navy was to say no. I then introduced the young man to another friend of mine, who was a senior leader in the Navy, to be his advocate. Two years later, the young man was cleared to live his dream as a Navy pilot.

Jodie: See? You're still making a difference for people in the Navy, even though you are no longer on active duty. I think it's pretty cool.
Reggie: Yeah, I do like that.
Jodie: Plus, it's starting to come full circle, which is also very rewarding. It's an added bonus you had never expected.
Reggie: Yes, it really is.

This was an exciting and liberating time for Jodie and Reggie as a couple. They were coming up on thirty years of marriage, but for the first time, it felt like their world was brimming with new possibilities. All of this was happening simultaneously with Jodie's personal growth and self-development journey. They soon realized they were not only the creators of their relationship but also of their entire reality. Jodie and Reggie became aware of their combined manifestation abilities and discovered that when they worked together and clearly understood what they wanted, they could attract whatever they desired even more quickly. They repeatedly asked themselves, "What do *we* want life to look like? What do *we* want to focus on? How would we like to proceed? What do we want our legacy to be?" It was a unique window of time where they actively focused on how their next chapter would unfold.

Jodie: Writing our next chapter is fun, but it can feel like a lot—like there is SO much we could do. So, how do we decide *what* to do?

Reggie: I agree. But we started by just asking ourselves these key questions: "What do we want? What brings us joy?" And we realized that, in addition to continuing to focus on our family, we still wanted to focus on service and making a difference.

Jodie: And travel and abundance and wealth creation. We also wanted to focus on our connection with each other because, even after all these years, I knew we could go deeper and take our relationship further.

Reggie: I pretty much thought we were good right where we were, and I wasn't sure where else we needed to go.

Jodie: [laughs] At times, I felt like I was exhausting you with my desire to be more connected.
Reggie: Well, it takes a lot of energy—that connection piece and strengthening our personal development.
Jodie: It does, but it's shown itself to be well worthwhile, right?
Reggie: It has, and I wouldn't have it any other way.
Jodie: I liked that we started to prioritize how we wanted to grow *together* and what we wanted to *feel* as a couple.
Reggie: I wanted to be sure we continued making memories together. I think this is when couples tend to separate—after such a long period of raising kids together and creating family memories, then their kids grow older and go on separate paths. The couple stops making memories with each other.
Jodie: How are we making memories now?
Reggie: I think it can be as simple as doing routine tasks, like paying bills or having coffee together in the morning.
Jodie: We do enjoy coffee together. I'm not a big fan of paying bills, but it is more enjoyable to do it with you than by myself, and it keeps us both more in tune with our money.
Reggie: We also listen to our morning meditation together before we even get out of bed.
Jodie: I'm barely awake when you turn on the meditation for us.
Reggie: It's the little things we prioritize and do together that encourage us to grow together every day.

———

HIGHER LOVE

Jodie and Reggie now had the capacity and ability to get more involved with their favorite non-profit. They served on the board and donated more time, money, and energy to the organization than ever before. They nourished themselves as individuals through new interests and greater self-care, which allowed more time and space to nourish their relationship. This was also a time when they were together, in the same place physically, more than they ever were before. After years of spending so much time apart, it now seemed like they had nothing but time to be together.

Jodie: You were around a lot more after you retired, and this was even before the COVID pandemic began.
Reggie: Yeah, that did help you prepare for lockdown.
Jodie: It was a bit of an adjustment, but it was really nice to have you around to help with the basics, like soccer practice and doctors' appointments. This was when you took over the laundry for me, which was amazing!
Reggie: Acts of Service is your love language.
Jodie: Ah! You remembered! Something that became very apparent during this time was our ability as a couple to make an impact. We realized that we are here to make a difference in lots of other ways, not just through military service or energy healing, and we could expand our platform.
Reggie: Ah, so is that why we started our podcast?
Jodie: Ha-ha! No, we started the podcast because of COVID, remember? And the fact that we couldn't renew

our vows in Italy for our thirtieth wedding anniversary like I had originally wanted.

Reggie: How could I forget?

Jodie: It was funny when people would ask, "So, what's your podcast about?"

Reggie: Just like they're now asking about this book.

Jodie: Exactly. The answer is pretty much the same: It's just us talking.

Reggie: I like to think that our audience is sitting at our kitchen table and listening in to our conversations. From raising kids to dealing with money to life challenges—you name it, we've experienced it and are willing to talk about it.

Jodie: For me, the unexpected part was that the podcast brought us closer together. It became one of the tools that deepened our relationship. There are things you've shared with me in the podcast that you had never shared with me before.

Reggie: Is that true?

Jodie: Yes! And whenever that happens, I just try to let you keep talking.

Reggie: To see what else you might discover about me?

Jodie: [laughs] Yep, and it works! The podcast creates a uniquely vulnerable space. When we are on "air," our authentic selves and our relationship shine through.

Reggie: What was it that your friend said?

Jodie: Oh, my friend who's never actually met you but listens to the podcast?

Reggie: Yeah, her.

Jodie: [laughs] After one particular episode, she told me, "When I finally meet Reggie, I'm gonna drop-kick him and hug him at the same time."

Reggie: I seem to have that effect on a lot of people.
Jodie: [laughs] You really do.
Reggie: But here's the thing: Everybody knows that my job on the podcast is to just talk. I'm just there to provide content, and sometimes, that content is a little unexpected or even controversial.
Jodie: You do have strong opinions.
Reggie: Doesn't that have something to do with my "Penthouse" Moon placement?
Jodie: [laughs] I think you mean your Gemini Moon. Once again, there is no such thing as a "Penthouse" Moon.
Reggie: See? I'm getting it.
Jodie: [laughs] Are you though? That was the arrangement for the podcast: I come up with topics, and you show up and talk. You have no idea what the topic is until we sit down and press Record.
Reggie: I just show up and be me, and you get what you get.
Jodie: You do prefer it that way.
Reggie: Are you going to talk about my "Penthouse" Moon again?
Jodie: Pretty much.
Reggie: How about they follow the QR code to learn more of that?
Jodie: Sounds good. And you still owe me that trip to the Amalfi Coast.
Reggie: Noted.

Higher Love: The Podcast grew, much like this book, from the space of wanting to share their story in the hopes that it will resonate with people on some emotional level. With over fifty episodes, the podcast provides a humorous and heartfelt look at daily life with Jodie and Reggie. They understand that while all couples face different challenges that might not look exactly like their own, there are always similarities and lessons to be learned. Through lively banter and conversation, Jodie and Reggie share their vulnerabilities with the audience in an honest and humorous way.

Jodie: There are lots of tools that have helped us reach this point in our lives and relationship, where we still really enjoy each other and want to spend more time together.
Reggie: Yep, and as I like to say, we may always love each other, but there's no guarantee we're always gonna like each other.
Jodie: *We* get to guarantee that we do—and it isn't by happenstance; it's by choice and choosing each other time and time again.
Reggie: It's also about staying open to our differences and all the opportunities life has brought us.
Jodie: Being *open* is key, and we've learned that we are truly the creators of our relationship. Even when one of us is going in a different direction, lagging behind, or facing a challenge, we still get to choose to be open with each other.
Reggie: We get to choose how we show up for each other daily.
Jodie: [laughs] It's an ongoing process—one you can enter into with excitement or dread!
Reggie: I choose excitement.

Jodie: Me too! What I find exciting about being with someone for over thirty years is the nuance and learning there is still so much more to experience together. I also like thinking about where we are going to be together in forty, fifty, sixty years.

Reggie: The best part is that even though I've been married to you for over thirty years, it doesn't feel that way because every day when you wake up, you're different than you were the day before.

Jodie: I like to keep on your toes.

Reggie: And I get to figure out that new person every single day. I wake up wondering what I'll have to figure out today and, more importantly, how I can make sure you still think being with me is a good idea.

Jodie: It's a *great* idea.

Reggie: Then I did my job for today.

In any relationship, the choices you make each day can either bring you a little bit closer to your partner or drive you further apart. This phase of exploring personal growth, as well as the growth as a couple, was enlightening for Jodie and Reggie. They saw the tangible, positive impacts of saying yes to each other every day. They explored new adventures, whether it was doing a podcast or writing a book together. It doesn't matter what the end results of the projects are; the value lies in the pursuit itself.

FINAL THOUGHT:

Life and relationships, especially marriage, are about growth and enjoyment. There's always more to discover about one another, making the journey of learning continuous and exciting. Instead of getting caught up in stress or taking things too seriously, it's essential to embrace fun and lightness. If something feels forced or unnatural, it's a signal to ease up and let things flow more organically. Building joyful connections involves both effort and the ability to relax, ensuring that love and partnership remain both meaningful and enjoyable.

KEY TAKEAWAY

Approach each day from the perspective that the person lying next to you is not the same person they were yesterday. Your mission, should you choose to accept it, is to give your partner a few reasons to believe they made the right decision in continuing to hitch their wagon to yours!

WHAT THEY WISH THEY HAD KNOWN: JUST SAY "YES!"

Physical pleasure can easily get lost amidst the wear and tear of everyday living. Especially in a long-term relationship, it becomes all too easy to fall out of physical connection and true intimacy with each other. For Jodie and Reggie, the status of their relationship *outside* the bedroom has always been a direct reflection of the health of their relationship *inside* the bedroom.

This exercise has been useful, particularly when they are feeling disconnected or wish they had more time and energy for intimacy. In a safe, loving, and respectful relationship, "Just Say Yes!" is a highly effective, fun, and playful exercise for getting things back on track—both inside and outside the bedroom.

How to Play: Choose one month—any month will do—where you both agree to "just say yes" to having sex every day. Yes! every day for an entire month. There is only one additional rule: *both* partners must climax each time you have sex. It doesn't count if only one partner gets there.

Believe it or not, there is actually a *lot* more to this exercise than just having sex. Jodie and Reggie discovered that this exercise removes the pressure of one partner feeling like they need to muster up the courage to initiate intimacy amidst the chaos of daily living. They also discovered that it totally alleviates the awkward possibility of being rejected by a partner you deeply love and respect. Furthermore, "Just Say Yes!" removes any of the power struggles that can become attached to sex in a long-lasting relationship. It injects a healthy dose of playfulness into pleasure and pure physical enjoyment of each other.

Wondering what could happen in your relationship if you knew that every day you would get to have sex *and climax* with the one you love? Try it!

Ready for more Jodie and Reggie?
Listen to *Higher Love: The Podcast*

SCAN THE QR CODE:

CONCLUSION: MARRYING WELL

Jodie: So, what do you think? Did we marry well?
Reggie: I know that I did. I think we're on an hour-by-hour, day-by-day determination on the answer to that one for you. Some would say that it's still up for debate.
Jodie: Good thing we've got many more years ahead of us to finalize it. But in all seriousness, our intention and goal was to share that "marrying well" can be done. You can be in a relationship for three decades with someone you love and someone you actually still like. How do you think we did?
Reggie: I think we did really good.
Jodie: Well, so do I. One of my favorite things is that day in and day out, *you* are the person I want to share everything with. You are the one I want to see and the person I want to spend most of my time with. I'm so grateful for this relationship and for what it has done for us and our children.

Reggie: And now *all* these people who've read our story will know that it's possible.

Jodie: It makes me really happy—all of it!

CHOOSING EACH OTHER, CHOOSING JOY

Happiness, just like being in a relationship, is a choice. You get to step into that choice every day, multiple times throughout the day, no matter what life throws at you. This doesn't mean that every moment of every day is pure happiness; it's not, nor is it supposed to be. Humans are here on this earth to feel and experience all types of feelings, but they are also here to let them go. At the end of the day, you can choose what is pulling you through. You get to decide how you want your relationship to play out and how you experience joy.

Reggie and Jodie's story began with their desire to walk through this life together. Since then, they have *decided* to do so with joy, not because it's always easy, but because that is what they chose. While it would be easy to get bogged down by everything that has happened *to* them, it's more empowering and enjoyable to realize that everything has happened *for* them. From that understanding, they can shift their focus, bringing the power back to their relationship, and the stress of the situation begins to thaw. They can release what no longer serves them.

Reggie: I like looking at the day-to-day aspects of happiness as being a choice. I wake up every day and ask myself, *How do I make Jodie want to choose me today? What are the*

things I can do to make that happen? Am I being open? Am I being supportive? Am I listening? Am I hearing her?
Jodie: I love and appreciate that you do that every day.
Reggie: I think you have to. You know, you say happiness is a choice—and it is—but I don't want to make that choice hard for you because of my actions or inactions.
Jodie: Those are powerful questions to ask. It speaks to our accountability with each other and in our relationship. It speaks about how we want to continue to show up for each other. That is such an important piece, and hopefully, our readers have gotten that awareness throughout this book.
Reggie: My hope for our readers is to even have a glimpse of what I get to experience every day: a relationship that is equal parts fairy tale and reality. The true adventure is keeping the fantasy alive and ensuring it is as "real" as reality itself.
Jodie: There will be challenges.
Reggie: But they can be overcome. And when you take the time to overcome them, you'll find that you're in the place where, thirty years later, you're still with a partner who curled your toes back in year one and will keep curling them for the rest of your life.

Jodie and Reggie hope that their story resonates with you in a meaningful way. They've achieved their goal if you've laughed, shook your head, or felt inspired. They feel honored to share their story with you. Come back to this book again when you need it. Share it with others. Enjoy the lessons and messages, and may you carry a nugget or two of goodness in your life.

REFERENCES

1. *Wabi Sabi Love: The Ancient Art of Finding Perfect Love in Imperfect Relationships* by Arielle Ford
2. *The Five Love Languages: How to Express Heartfelt Commitment to Your Mate* by Gary Chapman
3. *The Sacred Enneagram: Finding Your Unique Path to Spiritual Growth* by Christopher L Heuertz
4. *The Law of Divine Compensation: On Work, Money, and Miracles* by Marianne Williamson
5. *The Big Leap: Conquer Your Hidden Fear and Take Life to the Next Level* by Gay Hendricks
6. *The Four Spiritual Laws of Prosperity: A Simple Guide to Unlimited Abundance,* by Edwene Gaines
7. *The Four Agreements* by Miguel Ruiz
8. *The Untethered Soul: The Journey Beyond Yourself* by Michael Singer
9. *The Surrender Experiment: My Journey into Life's Perfection* by Michael Singer
10. *The Artist's Way: A Spiritual Path to Higher Creativity* by Julia Cameron
11. *Jesus Calling: Enjoying Peace in His Presence* by Sarah Young
12. *You Can Heal Your Life* by Louise Hay
13. *A Course in Miracles* by Foundation for Inner Peace

NOTES

OUR ROARING TWENTIES

i. boatex: party on a lake where everyone with boats arrive with drinks, food and music.

BAHRAIN AND BEYOND

i. In Human Design, a Manifesting Generator (MG) is one of the five energy types, combining traits of both Generators and Manifestors. Manifesting Generators are known for their multi-tasking abilities, high energy, and rapid adaptability.
ii. A decision-making strategy in Human Design that applies to Generators and Manifesting Generators (MGs) who have a defined Sacral Center but no emotional authority (i.e., an undefined Solar Plexus).

WE HOPE YOU ENJOYED READING OUR BOOK!

ACCESS YOUR FREE GIFTS

We would like to give you access to our YouTube channel with additional exclusive content and bonus features just for you!

SCAN THE QR CODE BELOW:

We appreciate your interest in our book and value your feedback as it helps us improve future versions of this book. We would appreciate it if you could leave your invaluable review on Amazon.com with your feedback. Thank you!

Made in the USA
Middletown, DE
11 September 2025

13064845R00113